"WIT & HUMOUR IN BUSINESS"

A Treasury of
International Quotations

William Davis

Other books by William Davis

Three Years Hard Labour
Merger Mania
Money Talks
Have Expenses, Will Travel
It's No Sin to be Rich
Money in the 80's
The Rich: a Study of the Species
Fantasy: a Practical Guide to Escapism
The Corporate Infighter's Handbook
The Super Salesman's Handbook
The Innovators
Children of the Rich
The Lucky Generation: a Positive View of the 21st Century
Great Myths of Business
How to be British
The Rich: A New Study of the Species
The Alien

Introduction

Business life would be dull without wit and humour. It helps to establish personal rapport; defuses anger; provokes reflection as well as laughter, and can be used to illustrate a point or support an argument. It is a vital ingredient of an after dinner speech.

You may be one of those fortunate people who are endowed with a natural talent for wit. If so, congratulations. But there is no reason why we should expect everyone in business to have that gift.

Few things are more embarrassing than having to listen to Executives who think that they are in the same league as professional comedians. They string together a series of jokes without any regard for the context or relevance, make a mess of it and wait for the laughter that doesn't come. Many reputations have been damaged by ill-judged efforts to be funny.

The art of the humorous speech is that it remains a speech, moulded to the theme of the event (and the audience) with every remark pertinent to the occasion. So long as humour has a point, a sense of direction, and is unlikely to offend, you will never be far off the target.

The best is often based on some item in the news; in Britain, self-deprecation also goes down well. In many years as a public speaker, I have always kept a close eye on the media, jotting down everything that strikes me as absurd. I have, for example, run a long campaign – in speeches, articles, and books – against the proliferation of jargon because so much of it is pretentious nonsense.

This book is mainly intended for the quick collaring of an apt quotation but also for browsing; it can add sparkle to a speech and is an antidote to stress, a tranquiliser without side effects. It helps to keep things in perspective. Most of the quotes are short - 'brevity is the soul of wit' – and many contain a nugget of wisdom. I have shunned the coarse, but of course all humour is subjective – what one person finds amusing leaves another stony-faced or hurt. There is plenty here for every occasion.

Some of the quotes will no doubt be familiar, especially if they are from renowned wits like Oscar Wilde, Mark Twain or Woody Allen. They are like old friends whose existence we are glad to be reminded of; others are new friends whose acquaintance we are glad to make.

Keep in mind that many well-known sayings do not necessarily represent strongly held personal views. Novelists, playwrights and scriptwriters put into the mouths of their characters thoughts and sentiments which are different from their own. It should also be noted that many date back to earlier times; I have included those which still seem relevant and both witty and wise.

One of the main problems for anyone who sets out to put together a collection is that it is often hard to pin down the original source. I have, time and time again, come across sayings attributed to a variety of people. (Mark Twain famously wrote that "Adam was the only man who, when he said a good thing, knew that nobody had said it before him".) I have followed an old rule: when in doubt leave out. This is why you will find that many of the quotes are not attributed to anyone. They come from a wide range of sources – books, plays, newspapers and magazines, television and the internet. Some are from interviews I have done as a financial journalist.

Michael Montaigne, a sixteenth century French essayist, said that *"I quote others only to better express myself."* So do I.

William Davis

ABILITY

The chief ability of an executive should be to recognise ability.

The capacity for getting into trouble and the ability for getting out of it are seldom combined in the same person. Sometimes it is more important to discover what one cannot do, than what one can do.

What one cannot, another can.

Executive ability is deciding quickly and getting someone else to do the work.

Everyone excels in something in which another fails.
Latin Proverb

They are able because they think they are able.
Virgil

Tis skill, not strength, that governs a ship.
Thomas Fuller

Natural ability without education has more often raised a man to glory and virtue than education without natural ability.
Cicero

Men take only their needs into consideration – never their abilities.
Napoleon Bonaparte

People are always ready to admit a man's ability after he gets there.
Bob Edwards

• • • • ACCOUNTANTS • • • •

Accountants invented actuaries so that they could laugh at someone else.

An auditor is an accountant who comes on the field after the battle is won and bayonets the wounded.

Three men apply for a job as an accountant.
They are asked one question: What is two times two?
The first two fellows get it right.
The third one replies:
"What figure did you have in mind, sir?"
He gets the job.

An actuary is someone who cannot stand the excitement of chartered accountancy.

An accountant is a man hired to explain that you didn't make the money you did.

• • • • ACHIEVEMENT • • • •

*To accomplish great things we must live as if we
were going to die.*

You can get almost anything accomplished if you
don't care who gets the credit.
Ned Hay

*The surest way to get a thing done is to give it to the
busiest man you know, and he'll have his secretary do it.*

We can continue to achieve if we don't
get too comfortable.

*The world is not interested in the storms you encountered,
but did you bring in the ship.*

It is not enough to aim, you must hit.
Italian Proverb

It is not the mountain we conquer but ourselves.
Sir Edmund Hilary

Nothing is ever accomplished by a reasonable man.
G Bernard Shaw

*Somebody is always doing what somebody else
said couldn't be done.*

The more a man talks about what he is going to do,
the less he talks about what he has done.

• • • • ACTION • • • •

Man who waits for roast duck to fly into his mouth
must wait for a very, very long time.
Chinese Proverb

Hoping won't make something happen.

Actions speak louder than words – but not as often.

I wondered why somebody didn't do something;
then I realised that I was somebody.

You can't build a reputation
on what you are going to do.
Henry Ford

Action is eloquence.

If there is no wind, row.

If your ship doesn't come in, swim out to it.

It is better to light a candle than curse the darkness.
Confucius

Well done is better than well said.
Benjamin Franklin

The actions of men are the best interpreters
of their thoughts.
John Locke

There are really only three types of people:
those who make things happen,
those who watch things happen,
and those who say: what happened?
Ann Landers

Never mistake motion for action.
Ernest Hemingway

I want to see you shoot the way you shout.
Theodore Roosevelt

People who know how to act are never preachers.
Ralph Waldo Emerson

Action springs not from thought but from a
readiness for responsibility.

Action will remove the doubt that theory cannot solve.
Chinese Proverb

Thunder is good, thunder is impressive;
but it is the lightning that does the work.
Mark Twain

• • • • ADVERSITY • • • •

Adversity reveals genius; prosperity conceals it.

Trouble is only opportunity in work clothes.

Adversity introduces a man to himself.

There is no education like adversity.

When it is dark enough, men see the stars.

In prosperity our friends know us;
in adversity we know our friends.

*The very difficulty of a problem evokes abilities
or talents which would otherwise, in happy times,
never emerge to shine.*
Horace

Every adversity carries with it the
seeds of a greater benefit.

*By trying we can easily learn to endure adversity.
Another man's, I mean.*
Mark Twain

Adversity has the same effect on a man
that severe training has on the pugilist –
it reduces him to his fighting weight.
Josh Billings

*Advise and counsel him. If he does not listen,
let adversity teach him.*
Japanese proverb

Every calamity is a spur and valuable hint.
Ralph Waldo Emerson

That which does not kill me makes me stronger.
Nietzsche

Learn to see in another's calamity the ills
which you should avoid.
Publilius Syrus

The worse the passage the more welcome the port.

• • • • ADVERTISING • • • •

Advertising is he fine art of convincing people
that debt is better than frustration.

In our factory, we make lipstick.
In our advertising we sell hope.
Charles Revlon

The philosophy behind much advertising is based on
the old observation that every man is really two men –
the man he is and the man he wants to be.
William Feather

Doing business without advertising is like winking
at a girl in the dark. You know what you are doing
but nobody else does.

I know half the money I spend on advertising is wasted,
but I can never find out which half.
John Wannamaker

Advertising is salesmanship in print.

Don't advertise; tell it to a gossip.

A clothing tycoon, Max Hart, summoned his advertising manager to complain about the latest campaign. "Nobody reads that much copy", he asserted. The ad manager begged to differ. "I'll bet you ten dollars, Mr. Hart, that I can write a whole newspaper page of solid type and you will read every word of it". The tycoon accepted the bet. "I won't have to write even a paragraph to prove my point", the ad man continued. "I'll just give you the heading: THIS PAGE IS ALL ABOUT MAX HART."

The codfish lays ten thousand eggs,
the homely hen lays one.

The codfish never cackles to tell you what she's done.
And so we scorn the codfish, while the humble hen we prize.
Which only goes to show you that it pays to advertise.

Advertising is like learning – a little is a dangerous thing.
PT Barnum

Promise, large promise, is the soul of an advertisement.
Samuel Johnson

You can fool all of the people all of the time of the advertising is right and the budget is big enough.
Joseph E Levine

The guy you've really got to reach with your advertising is the copywriter for your chief rival's advertising agency. If you can terrorise him, you've got it licked.
Howard L Gossage

Nothing except the Mint can make money
without advertising.
Macaulay

When the client moans and sighs
Make the logo twice the size
If he still should prove refractory
Show a picture of his factory
Only in the gravest cases
Should you show the client's faces.

An advertising man dies, and finds himself at the
Pearly Gates. St. Peter explains that they have a
special routine these days for his sort, who have to
spend a day in Heaven and one in Hell and choose
which they prefer. The ad man's day in Heaven is alright,
lying around on clouds playing harps, but a bit boring really.
The next day, in mortal terror, he gets into the lift and is
whisked down to Hell. And walks out onto a golf course,
on a beautiful spring day. All his old friends are there, and
they have a couple of rounds and then retire to a well
stocked clubhouse. Even the Devil turns out to be a
fine chap. The next day he cheerfully elects for Hell.
Down in the lift, and out into scenes of torment and
terror this time. Eternal flames, racks, boiling lakes.
And the Devil, grinning in the middle of it all.
"Where's the golf, where's the clubhouse?"
he asks as he is dragged off.
"You don't understand", says the Devil.
"Yesterday you were a prospect.
Today you are a client."

Echo men are very important in advertising.
They are men who follow in the wake of the
big executive and echo his sentiments
as they are expressed.
Fred Allen

Advertising is what makes you think you've longed for all
your life for something you've never heard of before.

Advertising is usually a trick to get you to spend money
by telling you how much you save.

Stopping our advertising to save money is like
stopping your watch to save time.

Her who calls a spade a spade won't last long
as an advertising copywriter.

The consumer isn't a moron; she is your wife.
David Ogilvy

You have a hard time finding an ad that isn't so busy
being different that it forgets to be an ad.
Par for the course is an eye patch on one eye and
a monocle on the other, topped by a beret
and bordered by a bear, riding backwards on a zebra,
wearing tails with red shoes, and using a violin
for a croquet mallet. When all around you are being
too, too clever then it's smart to be plain.
Arnold Gingrich

• • • • ADVICE • • • •

Advice is seldom welcome.
Those who need it most like it least.
Samuel Johnson

*Socrates was a Greek philosopher who went around
giving people good advice. They poisoned him.*

I am glad that I paid so little attention to good advice;
had I abided by it I might have been saved from
some of my most valuable mistakes.
Gene Fowler

To ask advice is nine times out of ten to tout for flattery.
Churton Collins

We ask advice, but we mean approbation.

*How we admire the wisdom of those
who come to us for good advice!*

Advice is information given by someone
who can't use it to someone who won't.

*Advice is what a person asks for
when he wants you to agree with him.*

An old man gives good advice to console himself
for no longer being able to set a bad example.
Josh Billings

Never trust the advice of a man in difficulties.

When we ask for advice we are usually looking
for an accomplice.

*He who builds to every man's advice
will have a crooked house.*
Danish proverb

Nothing is given so freely as advice.
French proverb

No enemy is worse than bad advice.

We may give advice, but we cannot inspire conduct.

*You will always find some Eskimos ready to instruct the
Congolese on how to cope with heat waves.*
Stanislaw Lec

Friendly advice has cost many a man his friend.

*If at first you don't succeed you'll find everyone
giving you advice.*

If you can tell the difference between good advice
and bad advice, you don't need advice.

Nothing is impossible to those who don't have to do it.

When a man comes to me for advice,
I find out what kind of advice he wants,
and I give it to him.

*The art of advice is to make the recipient
believe he thought of it himself.*

Don't be troubled if the temptation to give advice is
irresistible; the ability to ignore it is universal.

Don't take any advice – including this.

• • • • AGE • • • •

Strategies are okayed in boardrooms that
even a child would say are bound to fail.
The problem is, there is never a child in the boardroom.

The young do not know enough to be prudent,
and therefore they attempt the impossible,
and achieve it, generation after generation.
Pearl S Buck

I'm not young enough to know everything.
JM Barrie

You are old when you do more and more for the last time
and less and less for the first time.

I will never be an old man.
To me, old age is always fifteen years older than I am.
Bernard Baruch

Don't laugh at a youth for his affectations; he is only
trying on one face after another to find a face of his own.
Logan Pearsall Smith

The aged love what is practical,
while impetuous youth longs only for what is dazzling.

Many a man that can't direct you to a corner drugstore
will get a respectful hearing when age
has further impaired his mind.

Men of age object too much, consult too long,
adventure too little, repent too soon.
Francis Bacon

• • • • MIDDLE AGE IS: • • • •

When you are warned to slow down by a doctor
instead of a policeman.

When you begin to feel on Saturday night
the way you used to feel on Monday morning.

When you'd rather pay the piper than dance.

When all you exercise is caution.

When you go out and wind up all in.

When you are impressed not with the fact
that the grass is greener on the other side of the fence
but rather how difficult the fence looks to get over.

When we can do just as much as ever –
but would rather not.

How foolish to think that one can ever slam the door in
the face of age. Much wiser to be polite and gracious
and ask him to lunch in advance.
Noel Coward

There's one more terrifying fact about old people.
I'm going to be one soon.
PJ O'Rourke

Growing old is like being increasingly penalised
for a crime you haven't committed.
Anthony Powell

I have my eighty-seventh birthday coming up
and people ask what I'd most appreciate getting.
I'll tell you: a paternity suit.
George Burns

• • • • AGREEMENT • • • •

There is no conversation more boring
than the one where everybody agrees.
Montaigne

I have never in my life learned anything
from any man who agreed with me.
Dudley Malone

When people agree with me I always feel
that I must be wrong.
Oscar Wilde

I don't necessarily agree with everything I say.
Marshall McLuhan

• • • • AMERICA AND AMERICANS • • • •

America is so vast that almost everything
said about it is likely to be true,
and the opposite is probably equally true.
James T. Farrell

Americans like fat books and thin women.
Russell Baker

Losing is the great American sin.
John Tunis

...as American as English muffins and French toast.

When American life is most American
it is apt to be most theatrical.
Ralph Waldo Emerson

If American men are obsessed with money,
American women are obsessed with weight.
The men talk of gain, the women talk of loss,
and I do not know which talk is the more boring.
Marya Mannes

The pursuit of happiness, which American citizens
are obliged to undertake, tends to involve them
in trying to perpetuate the moods, tastes,
and aptitudes of youth.
Malcolm Muggeridge

America: a land of untold wealth.
Internal Revenue Service

Frustrate a Frenchman, he will drink himself to death;
an Irishman, he will die of angry hypertension;
a Dane, he will shoot himself;
an American, he will get drunk, shoot you, then establish
a million-dollar aid programme for your relatives.
Then he will die of an ulcer.
Stanley Rudin

Americans are like a rich father who wishes
he knew how to give his son the hardships
that made him rich.
Robert Frost

American enterprise;
the art of making toeless shoes a fashion
rather than a calamity.

America is a vast conspiracy to make you happy.
John Updike

Americans adore me and will go on adoring me
until I say something nice about them.
George Bernard Shaw

So much of learning to be an American is learning
not to let your individuality become a nuisance.
Edgar Freidenberg

The typical successful American businessman
was born in the country,
where he worked like hell so he could live in the city,
where he worked like hell so he could live in the country.
Don Marquis

*Americans hardly ever retire from business; they are
either carried out feet first or they jump from a window.*
AL Goodheart

• • • • ANGER • • • •

Never answer a letter when you are angry.
Chinese proverb

Beware the fury of a patient man.
John Dryden

Never forget what a man says to you when he is angry.

Anger is a bad counsellor.
French proverb

The greatest remedy for anger is delay.
Seneca

*An angry man is again angry with himself
when he returns to reason.
He is a fool who cannot be angry;
but he is a wise man who will not.*
English proverb

Anger punishes itself.

Growl all day and you'll feel dog tired at night.

A man is as big as the things that annoy him.

Anger makes me mad.

He never let the sun go down on his wrath,
though there were some colourful sunsets
while it lasted.
AA Thomson (of WG Grace)

*A man in a passion rides a horse
that runs away with him.*
Thomas Fuller

Anger without power is folly.
German proverb

The bare recollection of anger kindles anger.

Anger blows out the lamp of the mind.
Robert Ingersoll

*Many people lose their temper
merely from seeing you keep yours.*

Speak when you are angry and
you'll make the best speech you'll ever regret.
Ambrose Bierce

Act nothing in furious passion; it's putting to sea in a storm.
Thomas Fuller

• • • • ANXIETY • • • •

Anxiety is a thin stream of fear trickling through the mind.
If encouraged, it cuts a channel into which
all other thoughts are drained.

The thinner the ice, the more anxious
everyone is to see whether it will bear.
Josh Billings

I have a new philosophy.
I am only going to dread one day at a time.
Charles Schulz (Peanuts cartoon)

How much pain have cost us the evils which never happened!
Thomas Jefferson

We are often more frightened than hurt; our troubles
spring more often from fancy than from reality.

• • • • APOLOGY • • • •

An apology is saying the right thing
after doing the wrong thing.

Never ruin an apology with an excuse.
Benjamin Franklin

Man is the only member of the animal kingdom
that apologises – or needs to.

Humble pie is the only pastry that's never tasty.

It is a good rule never to apologise.
The right sort of people do not want apologies,
and the wrong sort take mean advantage of them.
PG Wodehouse

He (the businessman) is the only man who is
forever apologising for his occupation.
H.L. Mencken

*Never make a defence or apology
before you be accused.*
King Charles I

• • • • ARGUMENT • • • •

You have not converted a man
because you have silenced him.

A man never tells you anything until you contradict him.

There is nothing so annoying as arguing with
somebody who knows what he is talking about.

*If you win all your arguments
you'll end up with no friends.*

Silence is one of the hardest things to refute.

A long dispute means both parties are wrong.
Voltaire

I learned long ago never to wrestle with a pig.
You get dirty and besides, the pig likes it.
Cyrus Ching

*He said true things, but called them
by the wrong names.*
Robert Browning

I dislike arguments of any kind.
They are always vulgar, and often convincing.
Oscar Wilde

*What's the use of wasting dynamite
when insect powder will do.*

The art of being wise is the art
of knowing what to overlook.

*My sad conviction is that people can only agree
about what they're not really interested in.*
Bertrand Russell

There is no arguing with Johnson;
for when his pistol misses fire,
he knocks you down with the butt of it.
Oliver Goldsmith

*I like talking to a brick wall;
it's the only thing in the wold that never contradicts me.*
Oscar Wilde

Those who in quarrels interpose,
must often wipe a bloody nose.
John Gay

The only way to get the best of an argument is to avoid it.
Dale Carnegie

When an argument is over,
how many weighty reasons does a man recollect
which his heat and violence made him utterly forget?
Eustace Budgell

The aim of argument, or of discussion,
should not be victory but progress.
Joseph Joubert

Arguments only confirm people in their own opinions.

Never fall out with your bread and butter.
English proverb

When people are least sure, they're most dogmatic.
JK Galbraith

The only thing worse than being on the wrong side
of an argument is being on the right side
with no-one listening.

That a man may know how to argue is no proof
that he knows what he's arguing about.

I wouldn't mind him having the last word –
if only he would get to it.

The great charm in argument is really finding
one's own opinions, not other people's.
Evelyn Waugh

• • • • ATTITUDE • • • •

Whenever you are asked if you can do a job,
tell them, Certainly I can! –
and get busy and find out how to do it.
Theodore Roosevelt

We lost because we told ourselves we lost.
Leo Tolstoy

*So long as a man imagines he cannot do this or that,
so long is he determined not to do it; and consequently,
so long it is impossible to him that he should do it.*
Spinoza

Act like a lamb and the wolves will eat you.

*Blowing out the other fellow's candle
won't make yours shine any brighter.*

Your attitude, not your aptitude,
will determine your altidude.

*I was going to buy a copy of
The Power of Positive Thinking and then I thought:
"What the hell good would that do?"*
Ronald Shakes

• • • • BANKS • • • •

Banking establishments are more dangerous
than standing armies.
Jefferson

If you owe a bank enough money you own it.

A banker is a guy who charges you high interest
to borrow somebody else's money.

*A banker is a man who lends you an umbrella when the
weather is fair, and takes it away from you when it rains.*
Mark Twain

If money doesn't grow on trees, how come
banks continue to sprout branches.

• • • • BARGAIN • • • •

*These days you can buy anything
for only twice what it's worth.*

Something you cannot use at a price you cannot resist.

*Something so reasonably priced that they won't take
it back when you find out what's wrong with it.*

Necessity never made a good bargain.

A deal in which each party thinks he's cheating on the other.

Sometimes one pays most for the things
one gets for nothing.
Albert Einstein

• • • • BEGINNING • • • •

Well begun is half done.
Horace

If we wait for the moment when everything,
absolutely everything is ready, we shall never begin.
Ivan Turgenev

I start where the last man left off.
Thomas Edison

He who begins many things finishes but few.
Italian proverb

Nothing is more expensive than a start.
Nietzsche

Everything is difficult at first.
Chinese proverb

The creation of a thousand forests is in one acorn.
Ralph Waldo Emerson

A good beginning makes a good ending.
English proverb

• • • • BILLS • • • •

Happiness is getting a bill you've already paid,
so you can sit down and write a nasty letter.

Some people pay their bills when due,
some when overdue, and some never do.

It is only by not paying one's bills that one can hope
to live in the memory of the commerical classes.
Oscar Wilde

He that pays last never pays twice.
English proverb

• • • • BORES • • • •

A yawn is nature's way of giving the person listening
to a bore the opportunity to open his mouth.

Somebody's boring me – I think it's me.
Dylan Thomas

A bore is a man who deprives you of solitude
without providing you with the company.

A healthy male adult bore consumes, each year,
one and a half times his own weight
in other people's patience.

I am one of those unhappy persons
who inspire bores to the highest flights of art.
Edith Sitwell

A bore is a man who, when you ask him how he is,
he tells you.

Bore: a person who talks when you wish him to listen.

Each man reserves to himself alone
the right of being tedious.
Ralph Waldo Emerson

*It is the peculiarity of the bore
that he is the last person to find himself out.*
Oliver Wendell Holmes

● ● ● ● BOSS ● ● ● ●

Some people think Davis has a God complex,
but this is absurd. On the seventh day he works.
(Of Sammy Davis Jnr)

*You can't help liking the managing director –
if you don't he fires you.*

Whenever you're sitting across from
some important person, always picture him
there in a suit of long red underwear.
That's the way I always operation in business.
Joseph P Kennedy

*The eye of the master will do more work
than both his hands.*
Benjamin Franklin

At too many companies, the boss shoots the arrow
of managerial performance and then hastily paints
the bull's-eye around the spot where it lands.
Warren Buffett

Boss: One who's late when you're early
and early when you're late.

When I take a long time I am slow.
When my boss takes a long time, he is thorough.
When I don't do it, I am lazy.
When my boss doesn't do it, he is too busy.
When I do something without being told,
I am trying to be smart.
When my boss does the same, that is initiative.
When I please my boss, I am apple-polishing.
When my boss pleases his boss, he's co-operating.
When I do good, my boss never remembers.
When I do wrong, he never forgets.

• • • • BRIBERY AND CORRUPTION • • • •

A silver key can open an iron lock.
English saying

A friend that you buy with presents will be bought from you.
Thomas Fuller

The jingle of the guinea helps the hurt that honour feels.
Tennyson

A dog will not howl if you beat him with a bone.
Proverb

A refuseth the bribe but putteth forth his hand.
English proverb

A conscience which has been bought once
will be bought twice.

Public money is like holy water;
everyone helps himself to it.
Italian proverb

I just received the following wire from my generous Daddy:
"Dear Jack, don't buy a single vote more than necessary.
I'll be damned if I'm going to pay for a landslide."
John F Kennedy

Every man has his price.
Sir Robert Walpole

• • • • BUDGET • • • •

Merely a mathematical confirmation of your suspicions.

A budget is a formula for telling you
that you need a raise.

A budget is a sort of conscience which doesn't keep
you from spending, but makes you feel guilty about it.

Budgeting: a method of worrying
before you spend instead of afterward.

A device to tell you where your money should have gone.

*The trouble with the average family budget
is that at the end of the money
there's too much month left.*

Some people go over their budgets very carefully
every month, others just go over them.

A minister of finance is a legally authorised pickpocket.

• • • • BUREAUCRACY • • • •

Bureaucrats write memoranda both because they
appear to be busy when they are writing
and because the memos, once written,
immediately become proof that they were busy.
Charles Peters

*The only thing that saves us from bureaucracy
is its inefficiency.*
Eugene McCarthy

The longer the title, the less important the job.

A civil servant doesn't make jokes.
Eugene Ionesco

There is something about a bureaucrat
that does not like a poem.
Gore Vidal

Bureaucracy is a giant mechanism operated by pygmies.

Balzac

Bureaucracy is the layer, or layers of management
that lies between the person who has decision-making
authority on a project and the highest-level person
who is working on it full-time.
Herbert Rees

*The perfect bureaucrat everywhere is the man
who manages to make no decisions
and escape all responsibility.*
Brooks Atkinson

CAPITALISM

Under capitalism man exploits man; under socialism the reverse is true.

Isn't capitalism wonderful?
Under what other system could the ordinary man
in the street owe so much.

Capitalism works better than it sounds,
while socialism sounds better than it works.
Richard Nixon

Capitalism is what people do when you leave them alone.

Capitalism has been presented as a transistory
and conditional compromise:
the worst possible system, as Winston Churchill
once said of democracy, except for all the others.

• • • • CARS • • • •

It's not a cheaper car that people want.
It's an expense car that costs less.

These are difficult days for car manufacturers:
they're thinking up ways to make their products safer and
new names to make them sound more dangerous.

People on horses look better than they are.
People in cars look worse than they are.
Marya Mannes

There are no liberals behind steering wheels.
Russell Baker

A pedestrian is a man who has two cars – one being
driven by his wife, the other by one of his children.
Robert Bradbury

No other man-made device since the shields
and lances of the ancient knights
fulfils a man's ego like an automobile.
Lord Rootes

Car: a convenient place to sit out a traffic jam.

Classic car: a car so old it's paid for.

The more parking spaces you provide, the more cars
will come to fill them. It is like feeding pigeons.
Sir Hugh Casson

You cannot become what you want to be
by remaining what you are.

*The one unchangeable certainty is that nothing
is unchangeable or certain.*
John F Kennedy

It is not the strongest of the species that survive
nor the most intelligent, but the ones
most responsive to change.
Charles Darwin

*The art of progress is to preserve order amid change
and to preserve change amid order.*

Progress is impossible without change; and those who
cannot change their minds cannot change anything.
George Bernard Shaw

*There is no way to make people like change.
You can only make them feel less threatened by it.*

There is nothing permanent except change.
Greek proverb

To remain young one must change.

Never leave well-enough alone.

*It is the nature of a man as he grows older to protest
against change, particularly change for the better.*
John Steinbeck

Change is not reform, any more than noise is music.

In prosperity, prepare for change;
in adversity, hope for one.

If you want to make enemies, try to change something.
Woodrow Wilson

God grant me the serenity to accept things
I cannot change, courage to change the things I can,
and wisdom to know the difference.
Reinhold Niehbur

Be the change.
Mahatman Ghandi

Times change, and we change with them.
Latin proverb

If we want things to stay as we are,
things will have to change.

• • • • CHARACTER • • • •

Character is doing the right thing
when no-one is watching.
J.C. Watt

You can tell a lot about a man's character
by the way he eats jelly beans.
Ronald Regan

*A person reveals his character by nothing so clearly
as the joke he resents.*
GC Lichtenberg

Character is something you either have or are.

*Every man has three characters; the one he shows,
the one he has, and the one he thinks he has.*
Alphone Karr

A man never discloses his own character so clearly
as when he describes another's.
Jean Paul Rixhter

*Many a man's reputation wouldn't know his character
if they met on the street.*

Character is what you are; reputation is what you
try to make people think you are.

*Having a character that consists mainly of defects,
I try to correct them one by one, but there are limits
to the altitude that can be attained
by hauling on one's own bootstraps.*
Clive James

I'm told he's a decent sort when you get to know him,
but no-one ever has, so his decency is sort of secret.
Tom Stoppard

*The measure of a man's real character
is what he would do if he knew that he
would never be found out.*

Talents are best nurtured in solitude; character is
best formed in the stormy billows of the world.
Johann Goethe

*You can judge the character of a man by how he treats
those who can do nothing for him.*

A signature always reflects a man's character,
and sometimes even his name.
Spike Milligan

• • • • COMMITMENT • • • •

*People must believe that a task is inherently worthwhile
if they are to be committed to it.*

What is the difference betweeen a contribution
to a cause and a total commitment?
It's like bacon and egg – the chicken has made
a contribution but the pig is totally committed.

*Consider the postage stamp. It's usefulness consists
in the ability to stick to one thing till it gets there.*

• • • • COMMITTEES • • • •

A committee is a group of people
who keep minutes and waste hours.

*A committee is a collect of the unfit chosen from the
unwilling by the incompetent to do the necessary.*

A committee is a cul-de-sac to which ideas are lured
and then quietly strangled.

Nothing is ever accomplished by a committee
unless it consists of three members, one of which
happens to be sick and the other absent.

If Moses had been a comittee,
the Isralites would still be in Egypt.

A man who shows up punctually at a committee meeting,
is probably attending for the first time.

A committee is a group of people appointed to
find some innocent individual to do the work.

Committees have become so important nowadays
that sub-committees have to be appointed to do the work.

A camel looks like a horse
that was planned by a committee.

• • • • **COMMON SENSE** • • • •

Common sense is not so common.
French proverb

Common sense is instinct, and enough of it is genius.

Common sense is in spite of, not the result of, education.
Horace Greely

Fine sense and exalted sense are not half so useful
as common sense.
Alexander Pope

There is nobody so irritating as somebody with
less intelligence and more sense than we have.
Don Herold

• • • • COMMUNICATION • • • •

The single biggest problem in communication
is the illusion that it has taken place.
George Bernard Shaw

If you don't give people information
they'll make up something to fill the void.
Carla O'Dell

It is difficult to get a man to understand something
when his salary depends upon his not understanding it.
Upton Sinclair

Kindly inform troops immediately
that all communications have broken down.
Ashleigh Brilliant

The communicator is the person who
can make himself clear to himself first.
Paul Griffith

You can stroke people with words.
Scott Fitzgerald

If people around you will not hear you,
fall down before them and beg their forgiveness,
for in truth you are to blame.
Dostoevsky

The most important thing in communication
is to hear what isn't being said.
Peter Drucker

It ain't watcha say, it's the way howcha say it.
Louis Armstrong

Half the world is composed of people who have
something to say and can't, and the other half who
have nothing to say and keep on saying it.
Robert Frost

The best way to nourish the grass roots is with bullshit.

When the eyes say one thing and the tongue another,
a practised man relies on the language of the first.
Ralph Waldo Emerson

Words are, of course, the most powerful drug
used by mankind.
Rudyard Kipling

A trembling hand, like a clenched fist, can speak volumes.
Goethe

I told the traffic warden to go forth and multiply,
though not exactly in those words.
Woody Allen

A good head and a good heart are always a formidable combination. But when you add to that a literate tongue or pen, then you have something very special.
Nelson Mandela

• • • • COMPETITION • • • •

If you can't win, make the fellow ahead of you break the record.

The competitor to be feared is one who never bothers about you at all, but goes on making his own business better all the time.
Henry Ford

Every morning in Africa, a gazelle wakes up.
It knows it must outrun the fastest lion or it will be killed.
Every morning in Africa a lion wakes up.
It knows it must run faster than the slowest gazelle,
or it will starve.
It doesn't matter whether you are a lion or a gazelle –
when the sun comes up, you'd better be running.
African proverb

We throw all our attention on the utterly idle question whether A has done as well as B, when the only question is whether A has done as well as he could.

A horse never runs so fast as when he has another horse to catch up and outpace.

*Those who will only compete when they can dominate
are not actually competing at all.*
Thomas Paulman

• • • • COMPROMISE • • • •

It is better to lose the saddle than the horse.
Italian proverb

A lean compromise is better than a fat lawsuit.

Lots of times you have to pretend to join a parade
in which you are not really interested,
in order to get where you are going.
Christopher Morley

*One of the most important trips a man can make
is that involved in meeting the other fellow halfway.*

Better bend than break.
Scottish proverb

*A compromise is the art of dividing a cake in such a way
that everyone believes that he has got the biggest piece.*
Former German Chancellor, Ludwig Erhard

A compromise is a settlement by which each side
gets what neither side wanted.

*Of course heaven forbids certain pleasures,
but one finds the means of compromise.*
Moliere

Computers will never replace man entirely
until they learn to laugh at the boss's jokes.

*The real danger is not that computers will begin
to think like men, but that men will begin to think
like computers.*

A computer can do more work faster than a human
because it doesn't have to answer the phone.

*We seem to be approaching an advanced state in
human progress where people are perfect and anything
that's wrong is the fault of computers.*

Computers are definitely smarter than people.
When have you ever heard of six computers
getting together to form a committee?

Computers are useless. They can only give you answers.
Pablo Picasso

To err is human but to really foul up requires a computer.

*Computers can solve all kinds of problems
except the unemployment problem they create.*

When I'm around hard-core computer-geeks I wanna say:
"Come out, the graphics are great".
Matt Weinhold

Abandon all hope, you who press ENTER here.

The computer is a great invention. There are as many mistakes as ever but now it's nobody's fault.

They sacked a guy at the office because they found a computer that could do everything he could do. Sadly, when he told his wife, she went out and bought the same computer.

We had a terrible day at the office. The computers went down and everybody had to learn to think all over again.

Computers make it easier to do a lot of things but most of the things they make it easier to do don't need to be done.
Andy Rooney

The email of the species is deadlier than the male.
Stephen Fry

Getting information from the Internet is like trying to get a glass of water from Niagra Falls.
Arthur C Clarke

Computers are almost human, except that it never blames its mistakes on other computers.

Computers are fantastic: in a few minutes they can make a mistake so great that it would take many men many months to equal it.

The Internet is becoming the town square for the global villages of tomorrow.
Bill Gates

• • • • CONFORMITY • • • •

Conformity is the jailer of freedom and the enemy of growth.
John F Kennedy

The great majority of men grow up and grow old
in seeming and following.
Ralph Waldo Emerson

*Conventional people are roused to fury by departure
from convention, largely because they regard
such departure as criticism of themselves.*
Bertrand Russell

Oh let us love our occupations, Bless the squire
and his relations, Live upon our daily rations,
And always know our proper stations.
Charles Dickins

*Success, recognition, and conformity are the bywords
of the modern world where everone seems to crave the
anesthetizing security of being identified with the majority.*
Martin Luther King Jnr

No one can possibly achieve any real and lasting success
or get rich in business by being a conformist.
Paul Getty

• • • • CONSULTANTS • • • •

*A consultant is someone whose approval is sought
after a decision has been made.*

After the ship has sunk, a consultant knows
how it might have been saved.

*Consultant: an expert called in when nobody wants
to take the blame for what is going wrong.*

A consultant is someone who saves his client
almost enough to pay his fee.

If it ain't broke, don't fix it. Unless you are a consultant.

A consultant is a man sent in after the battle
to bayonet the wounded.

*Those that do, do.
Those that did but now don't, consult.*

• • • • CONTRACT • • • •

Knowledge is what you get from reading the small print
in a contract; experience is what you get
from not reading it.

The older you get, the slower to read a contract.

This contract is so one-sided that I am surprised
to find it written on both sides of the paper.
Lord Evershed

*A contract is an agreement where the size of the print
tends to contract the more you read.*

• • • • COURAGE • • • •

Fear that has said its prayers.

No one can answer for his courage
when he has never been in danger.

Courage is often just ignorance of the facts.

Let me win, but if I cannot win,
let me be brave in the attempt.
Special Olympics motto

It is easy to be brave from a safe distance.

Always do what you are afraid to do.
Ralph Waldo Emerson

When the mouse laughs at the cat, there is a hole nearby.
Nigerian proverb

Audacity augments courage; hesitation, fear.

"I'm very brave generally", he went on in a low voice
"only today I happen to have a headache."
Lewis Carroll

It is better to err on the side of daring
than on the side of caution.
Alvin Toffler

Success is not final; failure is not fatal;
it is the courage to continue that counts.
Winston Churchill

Courage is looking a saleslady straight in the eye
and saying you'd like something cheaper.

When we do a courageous thing it is heroic;
when someone else does it, it's foolhardy.

A man has to have a lot of courage
to admit that he hasn't any.

Courage is being scared to death
and saddling up anyway.
John Wayne

Courage is rightly esteemed the first of human qualities
because it is the quality which guarantees all others.
Winston Churchill

It is always brave to say what everyone else thinks.
George Duhamel

Many would be cowards if they had courage enough.
Thomas Fuller

If you don't dare say 'no' how will you ever dare to say 'yes?'

It is curious that physical courage should be so common
in the world, and mental courage so rare.
Mark Twain

• • • • COURTESY • • • •

A form of polite behaviour practised by
civilised people when they have time.

Good manners are made up of petty sacrifices.

All doors open to courtesy.

*Good breeding consists in concealing how much
we think of ourselves and how little we think
of the other person.*
Mark Twain

Politeness: the most acceptable hypocrisy.
Ambrose Bierce

The lie is the basis building block of good manners.

The test of good manners is to be patient with bad ones.

Manners maketh the fortune of the ambitious youth.
Ralph Waldo Emerson

The real proof of courtesy is to have the same ailment
as the other person is describing and not mention it.

*We cannot always oblige,
but we can always speak obligingly.*
Voltaire

Etiquette: learning to yawn with your mouth closed.

• • • • CRIME • • • •

*A criminal is a person with predatory instincts who has
not sufficient capital to form a corporation.*
Howard Scott

The only way to make sure that crime doesn't pay
is to have the government take over and run it.

*I was going to read the report about the rising crime rate –
but somebody stole it.*

A kleptomaniac is a person who helps himself
because he can't help himself.

*We enact many laws that manufacture criminals,
and then a few that punish them.*

We don't seem to be able to check crime, so why not
legalise it and then tax it out of business.
Will Rogers

Whoever profits by the crime is guilty of it.
French proverb

He who holds the ladder is as bad as the thief.
German proverb

*Most men only commit great crimes because of
their scruples about petty ones.*
Cardinal de Retz

Opportunity makes the thief.
English proverb

*It was beautiful and simple
as all truly great swindles are.*
O Henry

• • • • CRISIS • • • •

When written in Chinese, the word 'crisis' is composed
of two characters – one represents danger
and the other represents opportunity.
John F Kennedy

*If you can keep your head when all around you are losing
theirs, it's just possible that you haven't grasped the situation.*
Jean Kerr

There can't be a crisis next week. My schedule is already full.
Henry Kissinger

*If you can manage to stay scared all the time, you'll soon find
that these international crises won't bother you at all.*

The best way out is always through.
Robert Frost

He who smiles in a crisis has found someone to blame.

There's no problem that can't be fixed by a miracle.

*Chairman: last year I told you that we were teetering
on the edge of a precipice. I'm glad to say that today
we are going to take a giant step forward.*

• • • • CRITICISM • • • •

Don't find fault; find a remedy.
Henry Ford

A successful man is one who can lay a firm foundation
with the bricks that others throw at him.
David Brinkley

To avoid criticism, do nothing, say nothing, be nothing.
Elbert Hubbard

A critic is a man who knows the way
but can't drive the car.
Kenneth Tynan

Critics are like eunuchs in a harem:
they know how it's done, they've seen it done every day,
but they're unable to do it themselves.
Brendan Behan

Taking to pieces is the trade of those who cannot construct.
Ralph Waldo Emerson

Criticism should be like a sandwich.
If you want to motivate people,
slip the criticism in between layers of praise.

A critic is a legless man who teaches running.
Channing Pollock

They who are to be judges must also be performers.
Aristotle

Criticism comes easier than craftsmanship.

Silence is sometimes the severest criticism.
Charles Buxton

Even the lion has to defend himself against flies.
German proverb

How much better the world would be
if we let opportunity do all the knocking.

Critics are like brushers of other men's clothes.
English saying

If you stop everty time a dog barks,
your road will never end.
Arab proverb

• • • • CUSTOMERS • • • •

Consumers are statistics. Customers are people.

It is not the employer who pays the wages.
Employers only handle money.
It is the customer who pays the wages.
Henry Ford

*A grocery clerk, tired of his job, quit to become
a traffic policeman. After a few days a friend
asked him how he liked his new job.
He said: "The pay and hours aren't too good,
but at least the customer is always wrong."*

You can automate the production of cars but you
cannot automate the production of customers.
Henry Ford

About the only people who don't get customers coming back complaining are parachute manufacturers.

When you are skinning your customers, you should leave some skin on to grow so that you can skin them again.
Nikita Khrushchev

• • • • CYNIC • • • •

A cynic is not merely one who reads bitter lessons from the past; he is one who is prematurely disappointed in the future.
Sydney Harris

What is a cynic? A man who knows the price of everything and the value of nothing.
Oscar Wilde

A cynic is just a man who found out when he was about ten that there wasn't any Santa Claus and he's still upset.
James Cozzens

Cynics are only happy in making the world as barren for others as they have made it for themselves.
George Meredith

Cynic: a blackguard whose faulty vision sees things as they are, not as they ought to be.
Ambrose Bierce

Cynic: a sentimentalist on guard.

No man in his heart is quite so cynical as a well-bred woman.
Somerset Maugham

• • • • DEBT • • • •

Running into debt isn't such a bad thing.
It's running into your creditors that's so embarrassing.

It is hard to pay for bread that has been eaten.
Danish proverb

The borrower is servant to the lender.
Bible

*An acquaintance is a person we know well enough
to borrow from but not well enough to lend to.*
Ambrose Bierce

Live within your income even if you have to borrow to do it.
Josh Billings

Out of debt, out of danger.

Creditors have better memories than debtors.
English proverb

Debts and lies are generally mixed together.
Rabelais

When some men discharge an obligation
you can hear the report for miles around.
Mark Twain

*The moment you make a man feel the weight of
an obligation, he will become your enemy.*

One must have some sort of occupation nowadays.
If I hadn't my debts I shouldn't have anything to think about.
Oscar Wilde

I just need enough to tide me over until I need more.

Good news rarely comes in a brown envelope.

*We often pay our debts not because it is only fair
that we should, but to make future loans easier.*

A debtor is any person who has enough money
to make the downpayment.

*When some people pay their debts they often act as if
they were conferring a great favour on their creditors.*

There's nothing as short as a short-term debt.

*I don't owe a penny to a single soul –
not counting tradesmen, of course.*
PG Wodehouse (My Man Jeeves)

• • • • DECISION • • • •

My decision is maybe – and that's final.

A decision is what an executive is forced to make when he can't get anyone to serve on a committee.

There's nothing easier than making up your mind about some things, especially what you would do in the other fellow's place.

When I was a junior executive, the directors would always try and involve me in the decision-making process. Sometimes they even let me toss the coin.

A peacefulness follows any decision, even the wrong one.
Rita Mae Brown

Every great leap in your life comes after you have made a clear decision of some kind.

The die is cast.
Julius Ceasar

Decisions are easier when there are no choices left.

There is a point at which we have to make a leap of faith, the point after which the right decision becomes wrong because it has been made too late.
Dwight D Eisenhower

The qualities that make a good manager is deciciveness.
Lee Laccoca

All our final decisions are made in a state of mind
that is not going to last.
Marcel Proust

• • • • DELEGATION • • • •

Don't do anything someone else can do for you.

Executive ability is deciding quickly and
getting someone else to do the work.

When you do for a man what he can and should do
for himself, you do him a great disservice.
Benjamin Franklin

A real executive goes around with a worried look
on his assistant's faces.
Vince Lombardi

Guidelines for Beaureacrats:
1. When In charge, ponder.
2. When in trouble delegate.
3. When in doubt, mumble.

Don't tell people how to do things. Tell them what to do
and let them surprise you with their results.
George S Patton

Here lies a man who knew how to enlist the service
of better men than himself.
Tombstone of Andrew Carnegie

• • • • DIGNITY • • • •

One thing that cannot be preserved in alcohol.

The eagle does not catch flies.

It is easier to grow in dignity than to make a start.

*I know of no case where a man added to his dignity
by standing on it.*
Winston Churchill

Only man can be absurd for only man can be dignified.
GK Chesterton

*The only kind of dignity which is genuine is that
which is not diminished by the indifference of others.*
Dag Hammerskjold

• • • • DISAPPOINTMENT • • • •

Disappointments should be cremated not embalmed.

*Too many people miss the silver lining
because they're expecting gold.*
Maurice Scitter

Disappointment should always be taken as a stimulant,
and never viewed as a discouragement.

*Blessed is he who expects nothing,
for he shall never be disappointed.*
Pope

Disappointment is the nurse of wisdom.

• • • • DISCRETION • • • •

I have never been hurt by anything I didn't say.
Calvin Coolidge

When you shut out the room, you must not peep through
the keyhole. Either break the door down or go away.
Dag Hammerskjold

*What is called discretion in men
is called cunning in animals.*
Jean de la Fontaine

A wise man sees as much as he ought,
not as much as he can.
Montaigne

It is not good to wake a sleeping lion.

There's a time to wink as well as to see.
Benjamin Franklin

The better part of valour is discretion.
Shakespeare

Great ability without discretion
comes almost invariably to a tragic end.
Gambetta

*Your friend has a friend, and your friend's friend
has a friend; be discreet.*

The age of discretion is reached when you have learned to close your eyes to a situation before someone else closes them for you.

It is easy for a man to be indiscreet in his talk, but only up to a pint.

• • • • DOUBT • • • •

Who knows nothing doubts nothing.
French proverb

To believe with certainty we must begin with doubting.
Stanislaw I, King of Poland

Doubt makes the mountain which faith can move.

When in doubt, tell the truth.
Mark Twain

Galileo called doubt the father is invention:
it is certainly the pioneer.
Bovee

I love to doubt as well as know.
Dante

Our doubts are traitors and make us lose the good
we oft might win, by fearing to attempt.
Shakespeare

The only limit to our realisation of tomorrow
will be our doubts of today.
Franklin D Roosevelt

Doubt and mistrust are the mere panic of timid imagination,
which the steadfast heart will conquer, and the
large mind transcend.
Helen Keller

• • • • DREAMS • • • •

Some men see things as they are and ask why.
I dream things that never were and say, why not?
George Bernard Shaw

All men of action are dreamers.

If you can dream it, you can do it.
Walt Disney

To make your dream come true, you have to stay awake.

Everything starts as somebody's daydream.

Dreams come true; without that possibility,
nature would not incite us to have them.
John Updike

Dreamers exist to keep the dreams alive
until the non-dreamers are ready to dream.
Pierre LeClerc

If you have built castles in the air, your work need not
be lost; that is where they should be.
Now put the foundations under them.
Henry Thoreau

• • • • DRESS • • • •

*It is an interesting question how far men would retain
their relative rank if they were divested of their clothes.*
Henry Thoreau

Good clothes open all doors.

No fine clothes can hide the clown.

A well-tied tie is the first serious step in life.
Oscar Wilde

By the husk you may guess at the nut.
Thomas Fuller

The first thing the first couple did after committing
the first sin was to get dressed. Thus Adam and Eve
started the world of fashion, and styles have been
changing ever since.

Women's clothes: never wear anything that panics the cat.
PJ O'Rourke

There'll be little change in men's pockets this year.

You should never have your best trousers on when
you go out to fight for freedom and truth.
Henrik Ibsen

If Botticelli were alive today he's be working for Vogue.
Peter Ustinov

• • • • DRINK • • • •

What the sober man thinks the drunkard tells.

One of the disadvantages of wine is that it makes a man
mistake words for thoughts.
Samuel Johnson

Don't make your nose blush for the sins of your mouth.

He drank like a fish, if drinking nothing but water
could be so described.

I've formed a new organisation called Alcoholics Unanimous.
If you don't feel like a drink, you ring another member
and he comes over to persuade you.
Richard Harris

An honest man that is not quite sober has nothing to fear.

I am speaking to you tonight under a severe handicap.
I'm sober.

I must get out of these wet clothes and into a dry martini.
Alexander Woollcott

Friendships are not always preserved in alcohol.

There is a devil in every berry of the grape.
Koran

It (drink) provokes the desire,
but it takes away the performance.
Shakespeare

Alcoholic: someone you don't like who drinks
as much as you do.
Dylan Thomas

Never drink on an empty wallet.

I always keep a stimulant handy in case I see a snake –
which I also keep handy.
WC Fields

My dad was the town drunk.
A lot of times that's not so bad – but New York City?
Henry Youngman

Actually, it only takes one drink to get me loaded.
Trouble is, I can't remember if it's the thirteenth or fourteenth.
George Burns

I know I'm drinking myself to a slow death,
but I'm in no hurry.
James Thurber

He often sits up late working on a case of Scotch.

The bartender looked up and saw a pink elephant,
a green cat and a yellow snake at the bar.
"You're a little early boys", he said. "He hasn't come in yet."

The bubble winked at me and said
"You'll miss me, brother, when you're dead."
Oliver Herford on champagne

Better to pay the tavern keeper than the druggist.

Never drink anything without smelling it,
never sign anything without first reading it.

Wine improves with age – I like it more the older I get.

Any port in a storm.

Never dive into pools of depths unknown,
and rarely drink – if you are alone.

• • • • ECONOMICS • • • •

The instability of the economy is equalled only by
the instability of the economists.
John H Williams

If you're not confused, you're not paying attention.

A man can be forgiven a lot if he can quote Shakespeare
in an economic crisis.
Prince Philip

*If economists could manage to get themselves
thought of as humble, competent people, on a level
with dentists, that would be splendid.*
John Maynard Keynes

If all economists were laid end to end,
they would not reach a conclusion.
George Bernard Shaw

*An economist is a man who states the obvious
in terms of the incomprehensible.*

Making a speech on economics is a bit like pissing down
your leg. It seems hot to you but never to anyone else.
Lyndon B Johnson

*Trickle-down theory: the less than elegant metaphor
that if one feeds the horse enough oats, some will pass
through to the road for the sparrows.*
JK Gilbraith

I think the light at the end of the economic tunnel
is starting to flicker again.

*It's a recession when your neighbour loses his job,
it's a depression when you lose your own.*

As I interpret the president, we're now at the end of the
beginning of the upturn of the downturn.
John F Kennedy (when Senator)

*Economics is like being lost in the woods. How can you tell
where you are going if you don't even know where you are?*

Take care to be an economist in prosperity;
there is no fear of your not being one in adversity.

*Business slump: when sales are down 10 per cent
and sales meetings are up 100 per cent.*

An economist is a man who knows more about money
than the people who have it.

*When an economist doesn't know the answer,
he changes the problem.*

An economist is an expert who will know tomorrow why the things he predicted yesterday didn't happen today.

Economists are always half right in their forecasts of better or worse conditions, but they are never sure which half it will be.

Economists are people who see something work in practise and wonder if it would work in theory.
Ronald Regan

Give me a one-handed economist. All my economists say "on the one hand ..... on the other."
Harry Truman (when US President)

Economics is extremely useful as a form of employment for economists.
JK Galbraith

There are three types of economists in the world: those who can count and those who can't.
Eddie George (when Governor of the Bank of England)

• • • • EMPLOYEE RELATIONS • • • •

Industrial relations are like sexual relations. They should be between two consenting parties.

You can't shake hands with a clenched fist.
Indira Gandhi

Employees make the best product when they like where they work.

The latest argument at a works renowned for its management problems got senior executives so upset that they began to stab each other in the front.
Aneurin Bevan

Good industrial relations is showing people that they are not just employees but human beings you are interested in.

A trade union is an island of anarchy in a sea of chaos.

You can handle people more successfully by enlisting their feelings than by convincing their reason.

Remember that a man's name is, to him, the sweetest and most important sound in any language.
Dale Carnegie

If you scream at workers, you may not discover the real problem.

• • • • ENEMIES • • • •

Love your enemies.
At least they don't try to borrow money from you.

A man cannot be too careful in the choice of his enemies.
Oascar Wilde

Don't think there are no crocodiles because the water is warm.
Malayan proverb

Speak well of your enemies. Sir, you made them.

*I never thought myself beaten so long as I could present
a front to the enemy. If I was beaten at one point I went
to another, and in that way I won all my victories.*
Tennyson

There is nothing like the sight of an old enemy
down on his luck.
Euripides

He makes no friends who never made a foe.
Duke of Wellington

Man is his own worst enemy.
Cicero

A man's greatness can be measured by his enemy.

Love your enemies, for they tell you your faults.
Benjamin Franklin

His must ber a very wretched fortune who has no enemies.
Latin proverb

Enemies are so stimulating.
Katherine Hepburn

It's easier to forgive an enemy once you've got even with him.

Pay attention to your enemies, for they are the first
to discover your mistakes.

A strong foe is better than a weak friend.

There is no safety in regaining the favours of an enemy.

• • • • ENTHUSIASM • • • •

Nothing is so contagious as enthusiasm.
Samuel Taylor Coleridge

You can do anything if you have enthusiasm. Enthusiasm is
the yeast that makes your hopes rise to the stars. With it,
there is accomplishment. Without it there are only alibis.
Henry Ford

*If you aren't fired with enthusiasm,
you will be fired by enthusiasm.*

Leadership is leaving zest in your wake.
Tom Peters

*One man has enthusiasm for 30 minutes, another for 30 days,
but it is the man who has it for 30 years
who will make a success of life.*

What this country needs is more young people
who will carry to their jobs the same enthusiasm
for getting ahead that they display in traffic.

*We act as though comfort and luxury were the chief
requirements of life, when all that we need to make us
happy is something to be enthusiastic about.*

In things pertaining to enthusiasm, no man is sane who
does not know how to be insane on proper occasions.

*The worst bankrupt in the world is the man
who has lost his enthusiasm.*

I prefer the errors of enthusiasm to the indifference of wisdom.
Anatole France

The world belongs to the enthusiast who keeps cool.

• • • • ENVY • • • •

Envy is the tax which all distinction must pay.
Ralph Waldo Emerson

It is better to be envied than be pitied.
Herodotus

Let age, not envy, draw wrinkles on thy cheeks.
Sir Thomas Browne

Envy is a kind of praise.
John Gay

The envious die not once,
but as oft as the envied win applause.

Even success softens not the heart of the envious.
Pindar

A show of envy is an insult to oneself.
Yevgeny Yevtushenko

As iron is eaten away by rust, so the envious are consumed by their own passion.
Antisthenes

If there is any sin more deadly than envy,
it is being pleased at being envied.
Richard Armour

• • • • EQUALITY • • • •

All men are born equal,
but quite a few eventually get over it.

The defect with equality is that we only desire it
with our superiors.
Henry Becque

All animals are equal, but some are more equal than others.
George Orwell Animal Farm

The only real equality is in the cemetery.
German proverb

We clamour for equality chiefly in matters in which we
ourselves cannot hope to obtain excellence.
Eric Hoffer

The principle of equality does not destroy the imagination,
but lowers its flight to the level of the earth.
Alexis de Tocqueville

We are all Adam's children, but silk makes the difference.
Thomas Fuller

• • • • EUROPEANS • • • •

The French want no-one to be their superior.
The English want inferiors.
Alexis de Tocqueville

*How can you expect to govern a country
that has 246 kinds of cheese?*
Charles de Gaulle

The Germans always buy a platform ticket
before they storm a railway station.
Nietzsche

*When a Swiss banker jumps out of the window,
jump after him. There must be money to be made.*
Voltaire

An Englishman, even if he is alone,
forms an orderly queue of one.
George Mikes

*The Irish are a fair people –
they never speak well of one another.*
Samuel Johnson

It is commonly known that one of the worst things
for a Norwegian is to be taken by a Dane.

Among the Greeks every man is an actor.
Juvenal

An Englishman's mind works best when it's almost too late.

To be or not to be, that is the question.
But the question is badly formulated.
(If Shakespeare had been a Frenchman)|

A German businessman who had fallen on hard times
decided to commit suicide. He went to the roof of a
high building but hesitated whether to jump or not.
Instead of pleading with him not to give up,
as they would have done in Britain, several Germans
shouted "Jump, you coward." And he did.
Lord d'Abernon

Rule Britannia Britannia waives the rules!

I once wrote that in order to reach for the truth, the Germans
add, the French subtract and the English change the subject.
I did not include the Americans since they so often give the
impression that they already have the truth.
Peter Ustinov

When we are in trouble, we talk.
When the Walloons talk, they are in trouble.
Flemish joke

Beware of Greeks bearing gifts? Nonsense! Instead,
beware of being unprepared when the gifts are brought.

The English may not like music, but they absolutely love
the noise it makes.
Sir Thomas Beecham

It is unthinkable for a Frenchman to arrive at middle age
without having syphilis and the Croix de la Legion d'Honneur.
Andre Gide

*When an Englishman is totally incapable of doing
any work whasoever, he described himself
on his income-tax form as a "gentleman."*
Robert Lynd

It is never difficult to distinguish between a Scotsman
with a grievance and a ray of sunshine.
PG Wodehouse

Very little counts for less in Italy than the state.
Peter Nichols

There are three things to beware of: the hoof of a horse,
the horn of a bull, and the smile of an Englishman.
Seamus MacManus

If it was raining soup, the Irish would be out with forks.
Brendan Behan

The British tourist is always happy abroad as long as
the natives are waiters.
Robert Morley

*A French member of parliament went to sleep for half an hour
during a debate and when he woke up he found that he had
been made Prime Minister twice.*
Oswald Lewis

Heaven is a French cook, an English policeman,
a German engineer, an Italian lover and everything
organised by the Swiss. Hell is an English cook,
a French engineer, a German policeman, a Swiss lover,
and everything organised by the Italians.

The Irish people do not gladly suffer common sense.
Oliver St John Gogarty

Every St. Patrick's Day every Irishman goes out to find another Irishman to make a speech to.
Shane Leslie

• • • • EXAMPLE • • • •

Example is the greatest of all seducers.
French proverb

Few things are harder to put up with than the annoyance of a good example.
Mark Twain

Example is better than following it.
Ambrose Bierce

People seldom improve when they have no model but themselves to copy after.
Goldsmith

Example is the best precept.
Aesop

• • • • EXCELLENCE • • • •

Nobody gets to run the mill by doing run-of-the-mill work.

Learn to say 'no' to the good so you can say 'yes' to the best.

Striving for excellence motivates you;
striving for perfection is demoralising.

If you don't do it all excellently, don't do it at all. Because if it's not excellent, it won't be profitable or fun, and if you're not in business for fun or profit, what the hell are you doing there?
Robert Townsend

The society which scorns excellence in plumbing, because plumbing is a humble activity, and tolerates shoddiness in philosophy, because it is an exalted activity, will have neither good plumbing nor good philosophy. Neither will hold water.

It takes a long time to bring excellence to maturity.

Either dance well or quit the ballroom.
Greek proverb

*Life's like a play: it's not the length,
but the excellence of the acting that matters.*
Seneca

• • • • EXCESS • • • •

Excess on occasion is exhilarating. It prevents moderation from acquiring the deadening effect of a habit.
Somerset Maughan

*I hate to advocate drugs, alcohol, violence, or insanity
to anyone, but they've always worked for me.*
Hunter S Thompson

Minds, like bodies, will often fall into a pimpled,
ill-conditioned state from mere excess of comfort.
Montaigne

You cannot have everything.
I mean where would you put it?
Steven Wright

With all the unrest in the world, I don't think anybody
should have a yacht that sleeps more than twelve.
Tony Curtis, Some Like It Hot

It is just as unpleasant to get more than you
bargain for as to get less.
George Bernard Shaw

• • • • EXCUSES • • • •

Justifying a fault doubles it.

Excuses interest no-one except the competition.

Unwillingness easily finds an excuse.
Benjamin Franklin

An excuse is worse and more terrible than a lie;
for an excuse is a lie guarded.
Alexander Pope

Several excuses are always less convincing than one.
Aldous Huxley

Bad excuses are worse than none.
Thomas Fuller

One unable to dance blames the unevenness of the floor.
Malay proverb

• • • • EXECUTIVE • • • •

A man who can take two hours for lunch
without hindering production.

A man who talks to visitors
while the employees get their work done.

One who never puts off until tomorrow
what he can get someone else to do today.

A man who believes in sharing the credit
with the man who did the work.

A man who has an infinite capacity for taking planes.

The best executive is the one who has the sense enough
to pick good men to do what he wants done,
and self-restraint enough to keep from
meddling with them while they do it.
Theodore Roovevelt

• • • • EXPENSES • • • •

In Brighton she was Brenda, She was Patsy up in Perth,
In Cambridge she was Candida, The sweetest girl on earth.
In Stafford she was Stella, The pick of all the bunch,
But down on his expenses, She was Petrol, Oil and Lunch.

• • • • EXPERIENCE • • • •

Experience teaches you to recognise a mistake
when you have made in again.

When you are young, you are not experienced enough
to know you cannot possibly do the things you are doing.

Experience is what happens to you
while you are making other plans.

Good judgement comes from experience, and experience –
well, that comes from poor judgement.

We learn from experience. A man never wakes up
his second baby just to see it smile.

Experience is the name everyone gives to his mistakes.
Oscar Wilde

Experience is the best schoolmaster,
only the school fees are heavy.
Carlyle

After the event, even a fool is wise.
Homer

He jests at scars that never felt a wound.
Shakespeare

And others' follies teach us not,
Nor much their wisdom teaches;
And most, of sterling worth is what
Our own experience preaches.
Tennyson

One thorn of experience is worth a wilderness of warning.

Experience teaches us at the expense of our illusions.

Experience is one thing you can't get for nothing.

By the time a man learns to watch his step,
he isn't going anywhere.

Experience is what permits you to make the
same mistake again without getting caught.

Experience is what keeps a man who makes the same
mistake twice from admitting it the third time round.

Experience is a comb which nature gives to men
when they are bald.
Eastern proverb

He who has once burnt his mouth always blows his soup.
German proverb

He who has been bitten by a snake fears a piece of string.
Persian proverb

What is experience? A poor little hut constructed from the ruins of the palace of gold and marble called our illusions.
Joseph Roux

Experience is an expensive form of knowledge which we let others have the benefit of for nothing.

The trouble with experience is that it is always teaching you things you don't want to know.

Experience is the training that enables people to get along without education.

Experience dulls the edges of all our dogmas.
Gilbert Murray

A fool learns from his experience.
A wise person learns from the experience of others.
Otto von Bismarck

To know the road ahead, ask those coming back.
Chinese proverb

Education is when you read the fine print; experience is what you get when you don't.

• • • • EXPERT • • • •

An expert is one who knows more and more about less and less.

From 'Ex', a has-been and 'spurt' a drip under pressure.

Make three correct guesses consecutively
and you will establish youself as an expert.
Lawrence Peter

Beware of being marched in bold logic by the
priestly up the garden path.

If women do what efficiency experts do, it's called nagging.

Experts should be on tap but never on top.
Winston Churchill

An efficiency expert attended a performance of Schubert's
Unfinished Symphony and issued the following critique:

1. For most of the performance, the four oboe players
had nothing to do. They should be eliminated and
their work spread out over the entire orchestra.

2. Forty violins were playing identical notes. This seemed
unnessary, and this section should be drastically cut.

3. The horns repeated the passages already played
by the strings. If this duplication was eliminated,
the concern could be reduced by twenty minutes.

• • • • FACTS • • • •

Generally the theories we believe we call facts,
and the facts we disbelieve we call theories.

*To treat your facts with imagination is one thing,
but to imagine your facts is another.*

Facts do not cease to exist because they are ignored.
Aldous Huxley

The trouble with facts is that there are so many of them.

The fewer the facts, the stronger the opinion.

*There is no sadder sight in the world than to see
a beautiful theory killed by a brutal fact.*
Thomas Henry Huxley

First get the facts, then you can distort them at your leisure.
Mark Twain

The surest way to spoil a good story is by sticking to the facts.

Get the facts, or the facts will get you.

Comment is free, but facts are sacred.
CP Scott (In the Guardian)

A wise man recognises the convenience of a general statement, but he bows to the authority of a particular fact.
Oliver Wendell Holmes

• • • • FAILURE • • • •

*Show me a thoroughly satisfied man,
and I will show you a failure.*
Thomas Edison

Failure is a man who has blundered,
but is not able to cash in on his experience.

*If at first you don't succeed,
destroy all the evidence that you tried.*

Failure is the opportunity to begin again, more intelligently.
Henry Ford

*A man fails many times but he isn't a failure until
he begins to blame somebody else.*
J Paul Getty

There's only one way you can fail, and that's to quit.

Failure is the path of least persistence.

I have had a lot of success with failure.
Thomas Edison

Success covers a multitude of blunders.
George Bernard Shaw

When I was a young man I observed that nine out of ten
things I did were failures. I didn't want to be a failure,
so I did ten times more work.
George Bernard Shaw

Everyone pushes a falling fence.
Chinese proverb

He who never fails will never grow rich.

Never give a man up until he fails at something he likes.

There is the greatest practical benefit
in making a few failures early in life.
TH Huxley

There is always time for failure.
John Mortimer

Results? Why, man, I've gotten a lot of results.
I know 50,000 things that won't work.
Thomas Edison

Many of life's failures are men who did not realise
how close they were to success when they gave up.
Thomas Edison

We are all failures – at least, the best of us are.
JM Barrie

*I don't know the key to success, but the key to failure
is trying to please everybody.*
Bill Cosby

If at first you don't succeed,
find out if the loser gets anything.
Bill Lyon

• • • • FAME • • • •

*What a heavy burden is a name that has
become too famous.*
Voltaire

Fame usually comes to those who
are thinking about something else.
Oliver Wendell Holmes

*A celebrity is a person who works hard all his life
to become well known, and then wears dark glasses
to avoid being recognised.*
Fred Allen

The final test of fame is to have
a crazy person imagine he is you.

Fame is proof that people are gullible.
Ralph Waldo Emerson

Some are born great, some achieve greatness,
and some hire public relations officers.

Popularity? It is glory's small change.
Victor Hugo

Fame is nothing but the sum of all misunderstandings collected around a name.
Rainer Maria Rilke

It took me fifteen years to discover that I had no talent for writing, but I couldn't give it up because by that time I was too famous.
Robert Benchley

Fame is the thirst of youth.
Lord Byron

Fame is a magnifying glass.
English proverb

Fame is a constant effort.

• • • • FARMING • • • •

Farming is not really a business: it is an occupation.
William E Woodward

A farmer is always going to be rich next year.

A farm is an irregular patch of nettles bound by short-term notes, containing a fool and his wife who didn't know enough to stay in the city.
SJ Perelman

Farming looks mighty easy when your plow is a pencil, and you're a thousand miles from the cornfield.
Dwight D Eisenhower

A farm is a section of land on which if you get up early enough mornings and work late enough nights, you'll make money – if you strike oil.

One good thing about living on a farm is that you can fight with your wife without being heard.
Kim Hubbard

• • • • FATE • • • •

Whatever limits us, we call Fate.
Ralph Waldo Emerson

Lots of folks confuse bad management with destiny.
Kim Hubbard

Unseen, in the background, Fate was quietly slipping the lead into the boxing glove.
P.G. Wodehouse

If fate means you lose, give him a good fight anyhow.
William McFee

Fate leads the willing, and drags along the reluctant.
Seneca

We make our fortunes and we call them fate.
Disraeli

No-one knows what will happen to him before sunset.
Turkish proverb

• • • • FAULTS • • • •

People who have no faults are terrible;
there is no way of taking advantage of them.
Anatole France

The greatest of faults, I should say, is to be conscious of none.
Thomas Carlyle

If we had no faults we should not take so much pleasure in
noticing them in others.
La Rochefoucauld

A man without faults is a mountain without crevasses.
He is of no interest to me.
Rene Char

Certain defects are necessary for the
existence of individuality.
Goethe

None of us can stand other people having
the same faults as ourselves.
Oscar Wilde

We keep deceiving ourselves in regard to our faults,
until we at last come to look upon them as virtues.
Heine

He is lifeless that is faultless.
English proverb

• • • • FOOD • • • •

If you are ever at a loss to support a flagging conversation,
introduce the subject of eating.
Leigh Hunt

*The lunches of fifty-seven years had caused
his chest to slip down into the mezzanine floor.*
PG Wodehouse

Asparagus inspires gentle thoughts.
Charles Lamb

We lived for days on nothing but food and water.
WC Fields

Eat drink and be merry, for tomorrow we diet.

Diets are for those who are thick and tired of it.

Minutes at the table don't put on weight – it's the seconds.

*The one thing harder than sticking to a diet
is keeping quiet about it.*

Losing weight is a triumph of mind over platter.

Lunch Hollywood style – a hot dog and vintage wine.
Harry Kurnitz

I just love Chinese food. My favourite dish is number 27.

I could never learn to like her – except on a raft at sea with no other provisions in sight.
Mark Twain

I will not eat oysters. I want my food dead.
Not sick, not wounded, dead.
Woody Allen

Beulah, peel me a grape.
Mae West

I am not hungry; but thank goodness I am greedy.
Punch

No-one goes to that restaurant any more - it's too crowded.

The only food that doesn't go up in price
is food for thought.

He who indulges, bulges.

When you go to a restaurant, always ask for a table
near the waiter.

A gourmet is just a glutton with brains.
Phillip Haberman

The glutton digs his grave with his teeth.
English proverb

• • • • FOOLS • • • •

A properous fool is a grievous burden.
Aeschylus

Most fools think they are only ignorant.
Benjamin Franklin

A fool always finds one still more foolish to admire him.

Nothing is more humiliating than to see idiots succeed in
enterprises we have failed in.
Gustav Flaubert

A fool and his money are soon parted.
English proverb

The most artful part in a play is the fool's.
Cervantes

A man may be a fool and not know it, but not if he is married.
HL Mencken

There is no need to fasten a bell to a fool.
Danish proverb

A learned fool is sillier than an ignorant one.
Moliere

The fool has one great advantage over a man of sense –
he is always satisfied with himself.
Napoleon Bonaparte

A fool never admires himself so much as when
he has committed some folly.
Chinese proverb

Answer not the fool in his error, for thine attempts
to instruct him will arouse his hatred.
Arabic proverb

A fellow who is always declaring he's no fool
usually has his suspicions.
Wilson Mizner

Fool: someone who has been found out.

There was a time when a fool and his money
were soon parted, but now it happens to everybody.
Adlai Stevenson

• • • • FORECASTING • • • •

It seems to me that no soothsayer should be able
to look at another soothsayer without laughing.
Cicero

Predicting the future is, intellectually, the most disreputable
form of public utterence.
Kenneth Clark

Man prefers to believe that which he prefers to be true.
Francis Bacon

The rule on staying alive as a financial forecaster
is to give them a number or give them a date,
but never give them both at once.

Business, more than any other occupation,
is a continual dealing with the future: it is a continual
calculation, an instinctive exercise in foresight.
You can only predict things after they have happened.
Eugene Ionesco

*The only way to predict the future is to
have the power to shape the future.*

• • • • FORGIVENESS • • • •

Forgotten is forgiven.
F Scott Fitzgerald

*"I can forgive, but I cannot forget",
is only another way of saying "I cannot forgive".*
HW Beecher

God will pardon me; that's his business.
Heine

*Don't carry a grudge. While you're carrying the grudge
the other guy's out dancing.*
Buddy Hackett

The weak can never forgive. Forgiveness is
the attribute of the strong.
Mahatma Ghandi

Always forgive your enemies; nothing annoys them so much.
Oscar Wilde

It is manlike to punish, but godlike to forgive.
Peter von Winter

Bear and forebear.

• • • • FRIENDS • • • •

You learn in this business: if you want a friend, get a dog.
Carl Icahn

*A friend is always happy about your success –
if it doesn't surpass his own.*

It is important to our friends to believe that we are
unreservedly frank with them, and important
to friendship that we are not.

*Friendship is like a bank account. You can't continue
to draw on it without making deposits.*

The best way to lose a friend is to tell him
something for his own good.

He is a good friend who speaks well of me behind my back.

Make new friends, but don't forget the old ones.
Yiddish proverb

A friend not in need is a friend indeed.

It is easier to forgive an enemy than to forgive a friend.

Every man should keep a fair-sized cemetery
in which to bury the faults of his friends.

Friendship consists in forgetting what one gives
and remembering what one receives.

If you want to make a dangerous man your friend,
let him do you a favour.

That friendship will not continue to the end
which is begun for an end.

A friend is someone whom we can always
count on to count on us.

When you are down and out, something always turns up –
and it's usually the nose of your friends.

Try your friend with a falsehood, and if he keeps it a secret,
tell him the truth.
Italian proverb

A friend is someone who dislikes
the same people that you dislike.

Prosperity makes friends and adversity tries them.

• • • • FUTURE • • • •

He who does not look ahead remains behind.
Spanish proverb

Remember, today is the tomorrow you worried
about yesterday.
Dale Carnegie

The best way to be ready for the future is to invent it.
John Sculley

When all else is lost, the future still remains.

The future belongs to those who believe in
the beauty of their dreams.
Eleanor Roosevelt

The future has a habit of suddenly and
dramatically becoming the present.

The ability to plan for what has not yet hapened,
for a future that has only been imagined,
is one of the hallmarks of leadership.

Your successful past will block your visions of the future.

I never think of the future. It comes soon enough.
Albert Einstein

Don't waste time looking back.
Your eyes are in the front of your head.

The future is no longer what it used to be.

The future never just happened. It was created.

The trouble with the future is that it usually arrives
before we are ready for it.

There is no future in any job. The future lies in the man who holds the job.

You can deal with the future more clearly
if you don't focus on the next week.

It is futile to try to guess what products the future will want.
But it is possible to make up one's mind what idea
one wants to make a reality in the future,
and to build a different business on such an idea.
Peter Drucker

If you do not think about the future, you cannot have one.

GAMBLING

The surest way of getting nothing for something.

Horse sense is what keeps horses from betting on what people will do.

The best throw of the dice is to throw them away.
English proverb

He who gambles picks his own pocket.

It may be that the race is not always to the swift, nor the battle to the strong - but that's the way to bet.
Damon Runyon

Without danger the game grows cold.

A wager is a fool's argument.
English proverb

There is scarcely an instance of a man who has made a fortune by speculation and kept it.
Andrew Carnegie

• • • • GENEROSITY • • • •

Less of your courtesy and more of your purse.
Scottish proverb

Lavishness is not generosity.
Thomas Fuller

Generosity consists not in the sum given,
but the manner in which it is bestowed.

Generosity is the flower of justice.
Nathaniel Hawthorne

A small gift is better than a great promise.
German proverb

You never want to give a man a present when
he's feeling good. You want to do it when he's down.
Lyndon B Johnson

To give and then not to feel that one has given
is the very best of all ways of giving.
Max Beerbohm

There is a sublime thieving in all giving.
Someone gives us all he has and we are his.
Eric Hoffer

Gifts are like hooks.
Martial

• • • • GENIUS • • • •

When a true genius appears in the world,
you may know him by this sign, that the dunces
are all in confederacy against him.
Jonathan Swift

*The secret of genius is to carry to spirit of childhood
into maturity.*
TH Huxley

A genious is a talented person who does his homework.
Thomas Edison

In every work of genius we recognise our rejected thoughts.
Ralph Waldo Emerson

Talent does things tolerably well;
genius does them intolerably better.

Since when was genius found respectable.
Elizabeth Barrett Browning

Doing easily what others find difficult is talent;
doing what is impossible for talent is genius.
Henri Amiel

*The function of genius is to furnish cretins
with ideas twenty years later.*
Louis Aragon

Patience is a necessary ingredient of genius.
Disraeli

No great genius has ever been without some madness.
Aristotle

• • • • GOALS • • • •

Before you can score you must first have a goal.

A goal is nothing more than a dream with a limit.

Goals help you to overcome short-term problems.

Arriving at one's goal is the starting point to another.

Goal-setting is the strongest human force for self-motivation.

*If you don't know where you are going,
you might wind up somewhere else.*

• • • • GOLDWYN GEMS • • • •
(Quotes attributed to
immigrant studio boss Sam Goldwyn)

A verbal contract isn't worth the paper it's written on.

*That's the way with these directors, they're always biting
the hand that lays the golden egg.*

Our comedies are not to be laughed at.

It's more than magnificent, it's mediocre.

Let's have some new cliches.

Never let the bastard back into my room again –
unless I need him.

What we need is a story that starts with an earthquake
and works its way up to a climax.

We have all passed a lot of water since then.

I don't want any yes-men around me, I want everyone
to tell me the truth even if it costs them their jobs.

I'll believe in colour television when
I see it in black and white.

Tell me, how did you love my picture?

We're overpaying him, but he's worth it.

Gentlemen, include me out.

I had a terrific idea this morning, but I didn't like it.

Anyone who goes to a psychiatrist ought to
have his head examined.

You've got to take the bull between your teeth.

● ● ● ● **GOLF** ● ● ● ●

A handicapped golfer is a man who plays with his boss.

My golf is improving. Yesterday I hit the ball in one.

I could tell the previous speaker was a golfer by the way he held the mike with an interlocking grip.

Golf is so popular simply because it's the best game in the world at which to be bad.
AA Milne

The least thing upsets him on the links. He missed short putts because of the uproar of the butterfies in the adjoining meadows.
PG Wodehouse

I play golf in the low 80s. If it's any hotter than that, I won't play.
Joe E Lewis

In golf the ball always lies poorly; and the player well.

Golf is a good walk spoiled.
Mark Twain

Give me my golf clubs, fresh air and a beautiful partner, and you can keep my golf clubs and the fresh air.
Jack Benny

I have a bad swing, a bad stance and a bad grip, but my bank manager loves me.
Lee Trevino

Golf is like an eighteen-year-old girl with big boobs. You know it's wrong but you can't keep away from her.

I refuse to play golf with Errol Flynn. If I want to play with a prick, I'll play with my own.
WC Fields

Golf is the most popular way of beating around the bush.

What men do to relax when they
are too tired to mow the lawn.

You can always tell a golfer who is winning. He's the one
who keeps telling his opponent that it's only a game.

He plays a fair game of golf – if you watch him.

Well caddy, how do you like my game?
It's terrific, sir. Mind you, I still prefer golf.
Robert Mynd

The man who takes up golf to take his mind off his work,
soon takes up work to get his mind off golf.

Another thing to be grateful for is that many people
do their worst driving on golf courses.

As soon as a businessman takes up golf,
he becomes an executive.

I know I'm getting better at golf
because I'm hitting fewer spectators.
Gerald Ford (when president of the US)

• • • • GOSSIP • • • •

Gossip is when you hear something you like
about someone you don't.
Earl Wilson

I hate to spread rumours, but what else can you do with them.

*Gossip is what you say about the objects of flattery
when they aren't present.*
PJ O'Rourke

I know that's a secret, for it is whispered everywhere.
William Congreve

*There's only one thing in the world worse than being talked
about, and that is not being talked about.*
Oscar Wilde

A gossip tells things before you have a chance to tell them.

*I will never repeat gossip, so please listen carefully
the first time.*

Whoever gossips to you will gossip of you.
Spanish proverb

*Gossip always travels faster over grapevines
that are slightly sour.*

She has a nice sense of rumour.

*None are so fond of secrets as those who
do not mean to keep them.*
Charles Colton

Don't forget to tell everyone it's a secret.
Gerald Lieberman

"They say" is the biggest lie in the land.

Nothing travels faster than a rumour, especially one that doesn't have a leg to stand on.

No-one gossips about other people's secret virtues.
Bertrand Russell

He's my friend that speaks well of me behind my back.
Thomas Fuller

It is perfectly monstrous the way people go about, nowadays, saying things against one behind one's back that are absolutely and entirely true.
Oscar Wilde

I don't call it gossip, I call it "emotional speculation."
Laurie Colvin

• • • • GOVERNMENT • • • •

Government should not interefere with any business capable of failing by itself.

Washington is a small town on the Potomac surrounded completely by reality.
George Will

Any man who thinks he is going to be happy and prosperous by letting the government take care of him should take a close look at the American Indian.

You don't see me at Vegas or at the races throwing my money around. I've got a government to support.
Bob Hope

To make crime unprofitable, let the government run it.

The natural progress of things is for government to gain ground and for liberty to yield.
Thomas Jefferson

When you think of the government debt the next generation must pay off, it's no wonder a baby yells when it is born.

Almost any system of government will work if the people will.

Useless laws weaken the necessary laws.

Govern a great nation as you would cook a small fish. Don't overdo it.
Lao-Tzu

The only thing that saves us from bureaucracy is its inefficiency.

There's no trick to being a humorist when you have the whole government working for you.
Milton Friedman

A government that is big enough to give you all you want is big enough to take it all away.
Barry Goldwater

Many people consider the things government does for them to be social progress, but they regard to things government does for others as socialism.
Chief Justice Earl Warren

Whenever you have an efficient government you have a dictatorship.
Harry S Truman

• • • • GRATITUDE • • • •

The gratitude of most men is but a secret desire
of receiving greater benefits.
La Rochefoucauld

Next to ingratitude, the most painful thing to bear is gratitude.
Henry Ward Beecher

Gratitude is a duty which ought to be paid,
but which none has a right to expect.
Rousseau

*Blessed is he who expects no gratitude,
for he shall not be disappointed.*

Nothing tires a man more than to be grateful all the time.

Gratitude is the conscience of memory.

Gratitude is a debt which usually goes on accumulating
like blackmail; the more you pay, the more is exacted.
Mark Twain

• • • • GREED • • • •

If your desires be endless, your cares and fears will be so too.
Thomas Fuller

Big mouthfuls often choke.
Italian proverb

He would skin a flint.
John Berthelson

The covetous man is ever in want.
Horace

He is better with a rake than with a fork.
English proverb

I have one basic drive on my side they can't defeat – greed.
Frank Zappa

The entire essence of America is the hope to first make money – then make money with money – then make lots of money with lots of money.
Paul Erdman

• • • • GUESTS • • • •

A constant guest is never welcome.
English proverb

A guest sees more in an hour than the host in a year.
Polish proverb

My evening visitors, if they cannot see the clock should find the time in my face.
Ralph Waldo Emerson

When hospitality becomes an art, it loses its very soul.
Max Beerbohm

Killjoy was here.

Friendship increases in visiting friends,
but in visiting them seldom.
Thomas Fuller

No one can be so welcome a guest that he will not
annoy his host after three days.
Plautus

• • • • GUILT • • • •

He declares himself guilty who justifies himself
before accusation.
Thomas Fuller

A guilty conscience is the mother of invention.
Carolyn Wells

The guilty think all talk is of themselves.
Chaucer

It is only too easy to compel a sensitive human being
to feel guilty about everything.
Morton Irving Seiden

Everyone in daily life carries such a heavy, mixed burden
of his own conscience that he is reluctant to
penalise those who have been caught.
Brooks Atkinson

The offender never forgives.
Russian proverb

Guilt is always jealous.

A guilty conscience needs no accuser.
English proverb

HABIT

A shackle for the free.

Habits are first cobwebs then cables.
Spanish proverb

Habits will reconcile us to everything but change.

Habit, if not resisted, soon becomes a necessity.
St Augustine

One of the advantages of being disorderly is that one is constantly making exciting discoveries.
AA Milne

Forgive him, for he believes that the customs of his tribe are the laws of nature.
George Bernard Shaw

If you always do what you've always done, you'll always get what you've always got.
Ed Foreman

Habit creates the appearance of justice;
progress has no greater enemy than habit.

Get in the habit of breaking your habits.

Cultivate good habits – the bad ones all grow wild.

*Men fall into a routine when they are tired and slack: it has
all the appearance of activity with few of its burdens.*
Walter Lippmann

• • • • HASTE • • • •

Whoever is in a hurry shows that the thing he is about
is too big for him.
Lord Chesterfield

Make haste slowly.
Latin proverb

Three things only are well done in haste: flying from
the plague, escaping quarrels, and catching fleas.
Russian proverb

He sows hurry and reaps indigestion.
Robert Louis Stevenson

One of the most pernicious effects of haste is obscurity.
Samuel Johnson

Haste makes waste.
English proverb

Hurry: a visible form of worry.

Some people are always in a hurry, even when they don't know where they're going.

The man who never has enough time to do a job properly always has enough time to do it over again.

Being in a hurry seems so fiercely important when you youself are the hurrier and so comically ludicrous when it is someone else.

When you want to hurry something, that means you no longer care about it and want to get on to other things.

In the old days, if a person missed the stagecoach, he was content to wait a day or two for the next one. Nowadays we feel frustrated if we miss one section of a revolving door.

Wisely, and slow. They stumble that run fast.
Shakespeare (Romeo and Juliet)

• • • • **HEROES** • • • •

Show me a hero and I will write you a tragedy.
F Scott Fitzgerald

Every hero becomes a bore at last.
Ralph Waldo Emerson

We can't all be heroes because somebody has to sit on the curb and clap as they go by.
Will Rogers

The idol of today pushes the hero of yesterday
out of our recollection; and will in turn,
be supplanted by his successor of tomorrow.
Washington Irving

*Better not be a hero than work oneself up
into heroism by shouting lies.*
George Santayana

However great the advantages given us by nature, it is not
she alone, but fortune with her, which makes heroes.
La Rochefoucald

*The chief business of the nation, as a nation,
is the setting up of heroes, mainly bogus.*
HL Mencken

• • • • HIRING • • • •

Eagles don't flock – you have to find them one at a time.
Ross Perot

The best time to fire a person is before you hire them.

Everybody looks good on paper.

Don't bet on horses. Bet on jockeys.

Hiring is a manager's most important job.
Peter Drucker

*I am always looking for people who can do
a better job than I can.*
T Boone Pickens

Never hire your client's children.
David Ogilvy

*The first-rate man will try to surround himself with his equals,
or betters if possible. The second-rate man will surround
himself with third-rate men. The third-rate man will
surround himself with fifth-rate men.*
Andrew Well

The employer generally gets the employees he deserves.
Sir Walter Bilbey

• • • • HOLIDAYS • • • •

*If all the year were playing holidays –
to sport would be as tedious as work.*
Shakespeare

A good holiday is one spent among people
whose notions of the time are vaguer than yours.
JB Priestly

A perpetual holiday is a good working definition of hell.
George Bernard Shaw

You must have been warned against letting the
golden hours slip by. Yes, but some of them are
golden only because we let them slip.
Sir James Barrie

I am happiest when I am idle. I could live for months without performing any kind of labour, and at the expiration of that time, I should feel fresh and vigorous enough to go right on in the same way for numerous more months.
Artemus Ward

It is better to have loafed and lost
than never to have loafed at all.
James Thurber

Leisure: time you spend on jobs you don't get paid for.

He does not seem to me a free man
who does not sometimes do nothing.
Cicero

Leisure is the mother of philosophy.
Thomas Hobbes

One of the symptoms of approaching nervous breakdown
is the belief that one's work is terribly important.
If I were a medical man, I should prescribe a holiday
to any patient who considered his work important.
Bertrand Russell

*It is impossible to enjoy idling thoroughly unless
one has plenty of work to do.*
Jerome K Jerome

· · · · HOLLYWOOD · · · ·

In Hollywood if you don't have a psychiatrist
people think you are crazy.

Behind the phoney tinsel of Hollywood lies the real tinsel.
Oscar Levant

Hollywood is a place where people from Iowa
mistake each other for stars.
Fred Allen

*One producer was so impressed with the money made
by The Ten Commandments that he hired a team
of writers to come up with ten more.*

In Hollywood they shoot too much film
and not enough actors.

*Hollywood is where, if you don't have happiness,
you send out for it.*
Rex Reed

Shoot a few scenes out of focus. I want you to win
the foreign film award.
Billy Wilder, to a cameraman

Hollywood is an asylum run by the inmates.

In Hollywood, writers are considered
only the first draft of human beings.

*Hollywood is Disneyland stages by Dante. You imagine
purgatory is like this except that the parking is not so good.*
Robin Williams

Hollywood is a sewer – with services from the Ritz-Carlton.
Wilson Mizner

*You can tell the economy is booming again. Yes-men in
Hollywood are getting so independent they're only nodding.*

Hollywood – a place where you spend more money
than you make, on this you don't need,
to impress people you don't like.
Ken Murray

• • • • HONESTY • • • •

A shady business never yields a sunny life.

It's strange that men should take up crime when there
are no many legal ways to be dishonest.

The only disadvantage of a honest heart is credulity.

In business today, it's not the thief who can destroy
a company. It's the honest man who doesn't know
what the heck he's doing.

One cannot be a little dishonest – it's all the way or nothing.

If you are honest because you think that is the best policy,
your honesty has already been corrupted.

*It would be ingratitude in some men to turn honest
when they owe all they have to their knavery.*

I am afraid that we must make the world honest
before we can honestly say to our children
that honesty is the best policy.
George Bernard Shaw

Anger cannot be dishonest.

Honesty is a fine jewel, but much out of fashion.

Honesty is the best policy, but there are too few policyholders.

How desparately difficult it is to be honest with oneself.
It is much easier to be honest with other people.
Edward F Benson

*The liar's punishment is not in the least that he is not
believed, but that he cannot believe anyone else.*
George Bernard Shaw

Those who think it permissible to tell white lies
soon grow colour-blind.

No man has a good enough memory to make a successful liar.
Abraham Lincoln

Tell your boss what you really think about him
and the truth shall set you free.

• • • • HONOURS • • • •

*Some are born great, some achieve greatness,
and others have it pinned on them.*
George Ade

It is better to deserve honours and not have them
than to have them and not deserve them.
Mark Twain

When I want a peerage, I shall buy one like an honest man.
Lord Northcliffe

It is sure that those are most desirous of honour
or glory who cry out loudest of its abuse
and the vanity of the world.
Spinoza

Birds pay equal honours to all men.
English proverb

A king may make a nobleman, but he cannot make
a gentleman.
Edmund Burke

*Nobel Prize money is a lifebelt thrown to a swimmer
who has already reached the shore in safety.*
George Bernard Shaw

I don't deserve this, but then, I have arthritis
and I don't deserve that either.
Jack Benny

Honour is better than honours.
Abraham Lincoln

• • • • HOPE • • • •

We should not let our fears hold us back from
pursuing our hopes.
John F Kennedy

Hope, deceitful as it is, serves at least to lead us to the end of our lives by an agreeable route.
La Rochefoucauld

He fishes on who catches one.
French proverb

Hope for the best, but prepare for the worst.
English proverb

Hope is the poor man's bread.

At first we hope too much, later on, not enough.
Joseph Roux

Hope warps judgment in council, but quickens energy in action.
Bulwer-Lytton

There are no hopeless situations; there are only men who have grown hopeless about them.

Free hope from fear and you become a dreamer.

Hope – desire and expectation rolled into one.
Ambrose Bierce

He that does not hope to win has already lost.

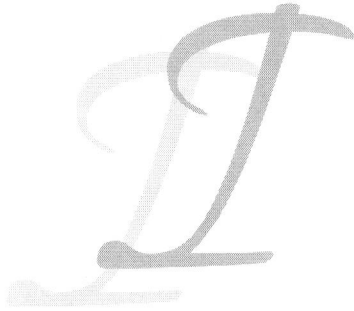

I

• • • • IDEAS • • • •

If you want to have a great idea, have lots of ideas.

If at first the idea is not absurd, there there is no hope for it.
Albert Einstein

Great ideas need landing gear as well as wings.

Many ideas grow better when transplanted into
another mind than in the one where they sprang up.
Oliver Wendell Holmes

*No army can withstand the strength of an idea
whose time has come.*
Victor Hugo

The idea that is not dangerous is not worthy
of being called an idea at all.

If you want to get an idea across, wrap it up in a person.

To some people a bright idea is beginner's luck.

I could not sleep when I got on a hunt for an idea,
until I had caught it; and when I thought I had got it,
I was not satisfied until I had repeated it over and over again,
until I had put it in language plain enough,
as I thought, for any boy I knew to comprehend.
Abraham Lincoln

Ideas are the raw material of progress. Everything first takes shape in the form of an idea. But an idea by itself is worth nothing. An idea, like a machine, must have power applied to it before it can accomplish anything.

A new idea is delicate. It can be killed by a sneer or a yawn;
it can be stabbed to death by a joke or worried to deal
by a frown on the right person's brow.

Every time a man puts a new idea across he finds ten men who thought of it before he did – but they only thought of it.

An idea isn't responsible for the people who believe in it.

It is better to entertain an idea than to take it home to live with you for the rest of your life.

No idea is no antiquated that it was not once modern.

No idea is so modern that it will not someday be antiquated.
Ellen Glasgow

A young man must let his ideas grow, not be continually
rooting them up to see how they are getting on.

The only sure weapon against bad ideas is better ideas.

• • • • IMAGINATION • • • •

*There are no days in life so memorable as those
which vibrated to some stroke of the imagination.*
Ralph Waldo Emerson

Imagination rules the world.
Napoleon Bonaparte

Reason can answer questions but imagination has to ask them.
Ralph Gerrard

Imagination is more important than knowledge.
Albert Einstein

What is now proved was once only imagined.
William Blake

Imagination grows by exercise and contrary to common
belief is more powerful in the mature than in the young.
Somerset Maugham

*Imagination makes a man think he can run
the business better than the boss.*

His imagination resembled the wings of an ostrich.
It enabled him to run, though not to soar.
Macaulay (of Dryden)

Anything one man can imagine, other men can make real.
Jules Verne

• • • • IMITATION • • • •

We are, in truth, more than half what we are by imitation.
Lord Chesterfield

The sense of inferiority inherent in the act of imitation
breeds resentment. The impulse of the imitators is
to overcome the model they imitate.
Eric Hoffer

Almost all absurdity of conduct arises from the
imitation of those whom we cannot resemble.
Samuel Johnson

A man never knows what a fool he is until
he hears himself imitated by one.
Sir Herbert Beerbohm Tree

We forfeit three-fourths of ourselves to be like other people.
Arthur Schopenhauer

It is better to fail in originality than to succeed in imitation.
Herman Melville

• • • • INDECISION • • • •

Nothing is so exhausting as indecision
and nothing is so futile.
Bertrand Russell

We know what happens to people who stay
in the middle of the road. They get run over.
Aneurin Bevan

Indecision is debilitating; it feeds upon itself; it is, one might almost say, habit forming. Not only that, but it is contagious; it transmits itself to others.
HA Hopf

They call him 'Jigsaw' because every time he's faced with a problem he goes to pieces.

His indecision is final.

Between two stools one sits on the ground.
French proverb

Nothing is more difficult, and therefore more precious, than to be able to decide.
Napeoleon Bonaparte

Half the failures in life arise from pulling in one's horse as he is leaping.

I don't mind telling you exactly what I think. I'm undecided.

If you want to make decision, then eliminate all the alternatives with the power of factual data. If you do not want to make decisions, then do us all a favour by staying out of the way.

One of these days is none of these days.
English proverb

I'd like to be a procrastinator, but I never seem to get around to it.
Chris Dundee

Procrastination is the thief of time.
Edward Young

Between saying and doing many a pair of shoes is worn out.
Italian proverb

One reason executives have trouble making decisions
is that they have less decision-making authority
than they wish to admit.

*There is no more miserable human being than the one
to whom nothing is habitual but indecision.*
William James

Once I make up my mind, I'm full of indecision.
Oscar Levant

He used to be fairly indecisive, but now he's not so certain.
Peter Alliss

• • • • INFLATION • • • •

Something similar to looking at your lifetime savings
through the wrong telescope.

*A state of affairs when you never had it so good
or parted with it so fast.*

The reason you can't take it with you –
it all goes before you do.

*The time when people who used to say money isn't everything
say it's hardly anything.*

Being broke with a lot of money in your pocket.

*The know inflation is out of hand when piggy banks
cost more than they hold.*

Inflation is a shot in the arm that leaves a pain in the neck.

*One of the principal troubles about inflation
is that the public likes it.*
Lord Woolton

Think of the inflation spiral as a gigantic corkscrew –
and think of yourself as the cork.

*Inflation is another one of those problems
that can't be cured by throwing money at it.*

Inflation may have been arrested, as the economists claim,
but whenever we go shopping it seems to be out on bail.

The cost of living is high, but it's worth it.

Inflation is the one form of taxation that can be
imposed without legislation.
Milton Friedman

*We have a love-hate relationship. We hate inflation,
but we love everything that causes it.*

Invest in inflation. It's the only thing going up.
Will Rogers

• • • • INHERITANCE • • • •

*The art of will-making chiefly consists of baffling
the importunity of expectation.*
William Hazlitt

Nobody talks more of free enterprise and competition
and of the best man winning than the man
who has inherited his father's store or farm.
C Wright Mills

*Say not you know another entirely till you have
divided an inheritance with him.*

He who inherits a penny is expected to spend a pound.

*A son can bear with composure the death of his father,
but the loss of his inheritance might drive him to despair.*
Machiavelli

I am spending my children's inheritance.

*It is a gorgeous gold pocket watch. I'm proud of it.
My grandfather, on his death bed, sold me this watch.*
Woody Allen

When you have told anyone you have left him a legacy,
the only decent thing to do is to die at once.
Samuel Butler

• • • • INSURANCE • • • •

Something that costs you thousands of pounds so that when you are dead you'll have nothing to worry about.

Insurance people present plans to keep you poor while you are alive so that you may die rich.

In every insurance policy the big print giveth and the small print taketh away.

I thought my group insurance plan was fine until I found out that I couldn't collect unless the whole group is sick.

"Don't let me frighten you into making a hasty decision, Frank. Sleep on it tonight. If you wake up tomorrow, call me."

Insurance salesman: "Now that you are married, I'm sure that you will want to take on more insurance on yourself". Young man: I don't think I need any more, I don't think she's that dangerous".

He said it was a matter of life and death. It turned out he was an insurance salesman.

Buy an annuity cheap, and make your life interesting to yourself and everybody else that watches the speculation.
Charles Dickens

Insurance is the business of protecting you against everything, except the insurance agent.

What really hurt Humpty Dumpty wasn't that he had a bad fall but that he had recently let his accident insurance lapse.

Accidents will happen.
Unless you have an accident insurance policy.

People who live in glass houses should take out insurance.

• • • • INTEGRITY • • • •

You don't turn integrity on and off. To have integrity
you must be like the fellow who uses a butter knife
when nobody is around.

The measure of a man's real character is what he
would do if he knew he would never be found out.
Macaulay

I either want less corruption, or more chance
to participate in it.
Ashleigh Brilliant

Character is doing what's right when nobody's looking.

These are my principles. If you don't like them I have others.
Groucho Marx

Character is a victory, not a gift.

In matters of style, swim with the current;
in matters of principle, stand like a rock.
Thomas Jefferson

Ethics stay in the preface of the average
business science book.
Peter Drucker

I ran the wrong kind of business, but I did it with integrity.
Sydney Biddle Barrows

You cannot drive straight on a twisting road.
Russian proverb

*Nothing so completely baffles one who is full of trick
and duplicity himself, than straightforward
and simple integrity in another.*
Charles Colton

• • • • INVENTIONS • • • •

We are more ready to try the untried when what we do
is inconsequential. Hence the remarkable fact that
many inventions had their birth as toys.
Eric Hoffer

*Inventor: a person who makes an ingenious arrangement of
wheels, levers and springs, and believes it civilisation.*
Ambrose Bierce

Inventor: an old-fashioned creator almost entirely
supplanted by research and development departments.

*We do owe a lot to Thomas Edison – if it wasn't for him,
we'd be watching television by candlelight.*
Milton Berle

Inventors and men of genius have almost always
been regarded as fools at the beginning
(and very often at the end) of their careers.
Dostoevsky

Name the greatest of all the inventors. Accident.
Mark Twain

Invention breeds invention.
Ralph Waldo Emmerson

Want is the mistress of invention.

Inventing is a combination of brains and materials.
The more brains you use, the less material you need.
Charles F Kettering

*The universe is full of magical things patiently waiting
for our wits to grow sharper.*

What we need is less inventions, and more mechanics
to service those we already have.

*The guy who invented the first wheel was an idiot.
The guy who invented the other three, he was a genius.*
Sid Caesar

There is no great invention, from fire to flying, that has
not been hailed as an insult to some god.
JBS Haldane

• • • • INVESTING • • • •

If you see a bandwaggon, it's too late.
James Goldsmith

Buy when everyone else is selling and hold until everyone else is buying. This is not merely a catchy slogan.
It is the very essence of successful investment.
J Paul Getty

Investing is not as tough as being a top-notch bridge player.
All it takes is that ability to see things as they really are.
Warren Buffett

It's a good deal easier to know what's going to happen than when it's going to happen.

There are two times in a man's life when he should not
speculate in stocks; when he can't afford it, and when he can.
Mark Twain

When you look at a stock you already own ask yourself every day "Would I buy this stock today?" If the answer is yes, then hold on or buy more. If the answer is no, then sell regardless of the value of the stock.
Bernard Baruch

How did I make my fortune? By always selling too soon.
Nathan Rothschild

Better to lose the anchor than the whole ship.

I've been burned in the stock market by picking up a hot tip.

People who play the market are often
led astray by false profits.

The only difference between the current stock market
and the Titanic is that the Titanic had a band.

I make a killing in the stock market. I shot my broker.

A friend in need is a friend who has been playing the stock market.

Buy land. They've stopped making it.
Mark Twain

I'm only working because of an accident. I got hit by a falling stock market.

Never invest your money in anything that eats or needs repainting.
Billy Rose

There is nothing so disastrous as a rational investment policy in an irrational world.
John Maynard Keynes

Fools rush in where angels fear to tread.

Old men are always advising young men to save money. This is bad advice. Don't save every nickel. Invest in yourself. I never saved a dollar until I was forty years old.
Henry Ford

Put all your eggs in one basket and then watch that basket.
Mark Twain

The bulls make money. The bears make money. But the pigs get slaughtered.
Wall Street axiom

JUDGEMENT

The good judgement of some people will never wear out.
They don't use it often enough.

*We judge ourselves by what we feel capable of doing; others
judge us by what we have done.*
Longfellow

Enthusiasm for a cause sometimes warps judgement.
William Howard Taft

*Most people suspend their judgement till somebody else
has expressed his own and then they repeat it.*
Ernest Dimnet

Evweryone complains of his memory,
but no-one complains of his judgement.

*The ultimate cynicism is to suspend judgement
so that you are not judged.*
Marya Mannes

Knowledge is the treasure, but judgement
the treasurer of a wise man.
William Penn

A hasty judgement is the first step to recantation.

• • • • KNOWLEDGE • • • •

The person who knows everything has the most to learn

To be conscious that you are ignorant
is a great step to knowledge.
Benjamin Disraeli

A little learning is a dangerous thing.
Alexander Pope

Knowledge is power.

He that knows little often repeats it.

Even a professor soon discovers how little he knows
when a child begins asking questions.

We are drowning in information but starved for knowledge.
John Naisbitt

The secret of business is to know something
that nobody else knows.
Aristotle Onassis

You never have to know all the answers because
you won't be asked all the questions.

You can know ten things by learning one.
Japanese proverb

You can always spot a well-informed man –
his views are the same as yours.

*Nothing annoys me more than a man
who thinks he knows it all – and does.*

The important thing is not to know more than all men, but
to know more at each moment than any particular man.

As knowledge increases, wonder deepens.

Knowledge and timber shouldn't be much used
till they are seasoned.

*Everything I know about this subject would fit into a nutshell
and still leave plenty of room for the nut.*
Lord Mancroft

If a little knowledge is dangerous, where is the man
who has so much as to be out of danger.
TH Huxley

Many shall run to and fro, and knowledge shall be increased.
Old Testament

A man should keep his little brain attic stocked
with all the furniture that he likely to use, and the rest
he can put away in the lumber room of his library,
where he can get it if he wants it.
Sir Athur Conan Doyle

In order that knowledge be property digested,
it must have been swallowed with a good appetite.
Anatole France

If we value the pursuit of knowledge, we must be free to
follow wherever that search may lead us. The free mind
is no barking dog, to be tethered on a ten foot chain.
Adlai Stevenson

Many men are stored full of unused knowledge. Like loaded
guns that are never fired off, or military magazines in times
of peace, they are stuffed with useless ammunition.
Henry Ward Beecher

LANGUAGE AND LANGUAGES

I speak Spanish to God, Italian to women,
French to men, and German to my horse.
Charles V

*English is a funny language. A fat chance and
a slim chance are the same thing.*

"Basta!" his master replied,
with all the brilliant glibness of the Berlitz school.
Ronald Firbank

*In Paris they simply stared when I spoke to them in French;
I never did succeed in making those idiots
understand their own language.*
Mark Twain

Slang is a language that rolls up its sleeves,
spits on its hands and goes to work.
Carl Sandburg

The great enemy of clear language is insincerity.
When there is a gap between one's real and one's declared
aims one turns as it were instinctively to long words
and exhausted idioms, like cuttlefish squirting out ink.
George Orwell

There is only one language that no-one speaks
like a native – Esperanto.

There are between two thousand and three thousand
languages spoken throughout the world,
not including that spoken by teenagers.

The letter is written in the tongue of the Think Tanks,
a language more dificult to mater than Basque or Navaho
and spoken only where strategic thinkers
clump together in Institutes.
Russell Baker

An unalterable and unquestioned law of the musical world
required that the German text of the French operas sung by
Swedish artists should be translated into Italian for the
clearer understanding of English-speaking audiences.
Edith Wharton

The great thing about human language is that it prevents us
from sticking to the matter in hand.
Lewis Thomas

We exchanged many frank words in our respective languages.
Peter Cook (as Harold Macmillan)

• • • • LAWYERS • • • •

The first thing we do, let's kill all the lawyers.
Shakespeare

Lawyers sometimes tell the truth, they'll do anything to win a case.

A poor man between two lawyers is like a fish between two cats.

It is a secret worth knowing that lawyers rarely go to law.

Laws are made to trouble people, and the more trouble they make the longer they stay on the statute books.

A lawyer is a learned gentleman who rescues your estate from your enemies and keeps it himself.
Lord Brougham

Where there is no will there is a way for the lawyers.

Woe be to him whose advocate becomes his accuser.

A society of men bred up from their youth in the art of proving by words multiplied for the purpose that white is black and black is white according as they are paid.
Jonathan Swift

Lawyer's houses are built on the heads of fools.
English proverb

I would be loth to speak ill of any person who I do not know deserves it, but I am afraid that he is an attorney.
Samuel Johnson

Laws, like houses, lean on one another.
Edmund Burke

The robes of lawyers are lined with the obstinacy of clients.
English proverb

*It is the trade of lawyers to question everything,
yield nothing, and to talk by the hour.*
Thomas Jefferson

Only painters and lawyers can change white to black.
Japanese proverb

*A lawyer is someone who will read a
10,000-word document and call it a brief.*

Talk is cheap – if lawyers don't do the talking.

*Lawyers make a living trying to figure out
what other lawyers have written.*
Will Rogers

My definition of utter waste is a coachload of lawyers
going over a cliff with three empty seats.
Lamar Hunt

*I get paid for seeing that my clients have every break
the law allows. I have knowingly defended a number
of guilty men. But the guilty never escape unscathed.
My fees are sufficient punishment for anyone.*
F Lee Bailey

If I were to give you an orange I'd simply say: "I give you this orange". But when the transaction is entrusted to a lawyer he puts down: "I hereby give and convey to you all and singular, my estate and interests, rights, title, claim and advantages of and in said orange, together with all its rind, juice, pulp and pips and all rights and adventages with full power to bite, cut and otherwise eat the same, or give the same away with or without the rind, skin, juice, pulp or pips, anything herein before and herein after or in any other deed, or deeds, instruments of whatever nature or kind whatsoever to the contrary in anywise notwithstanding ...."
Then a couple of smart lawyers come along
and take it away from you.

My son works for a law firm. He makes loopholes.

A jury consists of twelve persons chosen to decide
who has the better lawyer.

I don't know as I want a lawyer to tell me what I cannot do.
I hire him to tell me how to do what I want to do.
JP Morgan

One listens to one's lawyer prattle on as long as one
can stand it and then signed where indic-ted.
Alexander Woolcott

A lawyer is a man who helps you get what's coming to him.

Old lawyers never die, they just lose their appeal.

Talk is cheap, until you call a lawyer.

Lawyer: to save the state the expense of a trial,
Your Honour, my client has escaped.

99 per cent of lawyers give the rest a bad name.

• • • • LEADERSHIP • • • •

A leader takes people where they want to go.
A good leader takes people where they don't necessarily
want to go but ought to be.

*One of the tests of leadership is the ability to recognise
a problem before it becomes an emergency.*

People buy into the leader before they buy into the vision.

*Leadership is the ability to decide what is to be done
and then get others to want to do it.*
Dwight D Eisenhower

There are no bad soldiers only bad officers.
Napoleon Bonaparte

Without a shepherd, sheep are not a flock.
Russian proverb

It is always a great mistake to command when
you are not sure you will be obeyed.
Honore, Compte de Mirabeau

There is no trick to being a captain as long as the sea is calm.

A good leader can't get too far ahead of his followers.
FD Roosevelt

*Something is happening in our country. We aren't
producing leaders like we used to. A new chief executive
officer today, exhausted by the climb to the peak,
falls down on the mountaintop and goes to sleep.*
Robert Townsend

You manage things; you lead people.

The graveyards are full of indispensable men.
Charles de Gaulle

A good leader is a person who takes a little more
than his share of the blame and a little less
than his share of the credit.

*Keep your fears to yourself,
but share your courage with others.*
Robert Louis Stevenson

For if the trumpet give an uncertain sound,
who shall prepare himself to the battle?
Bible

*The final test of a leader is the feeling that you have
when you leave his presence after a conference.
Have you a feeling of uplift and confidence.*
Field Marshall Montgomery

You do not lead by hitting people over the head –
that's assault not leadership.
Dwight D Eisenhower

I must follow them. I am their leader.
Andrew Bonar Law, former Conservative Prime Minister

If you've got them by the balls,
their hearts and minds will follow.
Lyndon B Johnson

Men will follow him anywhere – out of curiosity.

A leader is a dealer in hope.
Napoleon Bonaparte

*The leader, mingling with the vulgar host,
is in the common mass of matter lost.*
Homer

The weakness of the many makes the leader possible.
Elbert Hubbard

• • • • LETTERS • • • •

*I have made this letter longer than usual because
I haven't had time to make it shorter.*
Pascal

A man seldom puts his authentic self into a letter.
He writes it to amuse a friend or get rid of a social
or business obligation, which is to say; a nuisance.
HL Mencken

*One of the pleasures of reading old letters is the
knowledge that they needed no answer.*
Lord Byron

The great secret in life is not to open your letters for a fortnight. At the expiration of that period you will find that nearly all of them have answered themselves.
Arthur Binstead

*They prosper who burn in the morning
the letters they wrote overnight.*

• • • • LUCK • • • •

Luck seems to have a peculiar attachment to work.

*Throw a lucky man into the sea, and he will come up with a
fish in his mouth.*
Arab proverb

The only sure thing about luck is that it will change.

A rabbit's foot may be lucky, but the original owner wasn't.

The only good luck many great men ever had was being born with the ability and determination to overcome bad luck.

*It often amazes me to hear men impute all their misfortune to
fate, luck, or destiny, whilst their successes or good fortune they
ascribe to their own sagacity, cleverness or penetration.*
Samuel Taylor Coleridge

Good luck is a lazy man's estimate of a worker's success.

A pound of pluck is worth a ton of luck.

Luck never made a man wise.
Seneca

Not a man alive has so much luck that he can play with it.
William Butler Yeates

Luck is not something you can mention in the presence of self-made men.
EB White

If it weren't for bad luck I wouldn't have any luck at all.
Dick Gregory

• • • • MANAGEMENT • • • •

Good management consists in showing average people
how to do the work of superior people.
John D Rockerfeller

*It's easy to get good players. Getting them to play together,
that's the hard part.*

Most business failures do not stem from bad times.
They come from poor management, and bad times
just precipitate the crisis.

*There are times when even the best manager is like the
little boy with the big dog waiting to see where the dog
wants to go so he can take him there.*
Lee Iacocca

If you can't get people to accept ideas because they're
sound, and if you are not willing to accept an idea because
it's sound, then you're really not a good manager.

Managers: people who take responsibility when things go right.

Lots of people confuse bad management with destiny.

*So much of what we call management consists
in making it difficult for people to work.*
Peter Drucker

• • • • MARKETING • • • •

Marketing is an attitude not a department.

*A man's success in business today depends upon his power
of getting people to believe he has something they want.*

The only way to covert a heathen is to travel into the jungle.

*Marketing is creating a condition that allows the buyer
to convince himself to buy.*

A good marketing strategy is to find a gap
in a market that already exists.

*There is more similarity in the marketing challenge of selling
a precious painting by Degas and a frosted mug of root beer
than you ever thought possible.*
Alfred Taubman (owner of Sotheby's)

• • • • MEASUREMENT • • • •

I am one of those unpraised, unrewarded millions without
whom statistics would be a bankrupt science. It is we who
are born, who marry, who die, in constant ratios.
Logan Pearsall Smith

Not everything that counts can be counted,
and not everything that can be counted, counts.

You can't measure the whole world with your own yardstick.
Yiddish proverb

Never measure the height of a mountain until you
have reached the top. Then you will see how low it was.
Dag Hammarskjold

He uses statistics as a drunken man uses lamp-posts –
for support rather than illumination.

Smoking is one of the leading causes of statistics.

Statistician: a man who draws a mathematically precise line
from an unwarranted assumption to a foregone conclusion.

There are no facts, only interpretations.
Nietzsche

Statistics are like loose women; once you get your hands
on them you can do anything you like with them.

Statistics are like a bikini. What they reveal is suggestive,
but what they conceal is vital.
Aaron Levenstein

There are two kinds of statistics; the kind you look up
and the kind you make up.
Rex Stout

• • • • MEDICINE AND DOCTORS • • • •

It is a poor doctor who cannot prescribe an
expensive cure for a rich patient.
Sydney Tremayne

One doctor makes work for another.

We've made great medical progress in the last generation.
What used to be merely an itch is now an allergy.

Mary had a little lamb. The doctor fainted.

Asthma is a disease that has practically the same symptoms
as passion, except that with asthma it lasts longer.

A psychiatrist is a man who asks you a lot of expensive
questions your wife asks you for nothing.

Show me a sane man and I will cure him for you.
Carl Jung

The art of medicine consists in amusing the patient
while Nature effects the cure.
Voltaire

There's another advantage of being poor –
a doctor will cure you faster.
Kim Hubbard

The desire to take medicine is perhaps the greatest feature
which distinguishes us from animals.
William Osler

Our doctor would never really operate unless it was absolutely necessary. He was just in that way. If he didn't need the money, he wouldn't lay a hand on you.
Herb Shriner

Some doctors tell their patients the worst –
others mail them the bill.

*Doctors are becoming easier to find these days.
Most of the caddies have portable phones.*

The physician must have at his command a certain ready wit,
as dourness is repulsive both to the healthy and to the sick.
Hippocrates

A minor operation: one performed on somebody else.

The purse of the patient protracts his cure.

Only a fool will make a doctor his heir.
Russian proverb

• • • • MEETINGS • • • •

Meetings are indispensable when you don't want
to do anything.
John Kenneth Galbraith

*Why do we take notes of meetings that last for hours
and call them minutes?*

Show me a person who likes to go to meetings and
I'll show you a person who doesn't have enough to do.

I always come to meetings with a problem.
I always leave with a briefing and a problem.

A conference is a gathering of important people who singly can do nothing but together can decide that nothing can be done.

Every discussion in a meeting has a diminishing curve of interest. The longer the discussion goes on, the fewer people will be interested in it.
Mark McCormack

Conferences are primarily a means of enabling people with some common interests to present a united front against the outside world.

If a manger spends more than 25 per cent of his time in meetings it is a sign of poor organisation.
Peter Drucker

Conference: a meeting at which people talk about what they should be doing.

You know, if an orange and an apple went into conference consultations, it might come out a pear.
Ronald Reagan

Parkinsons's Law of Triviality: The time spent on any item on the agenda will be in inverse proportion to the sum involved.
C Northcote Parkinson

The reason that everybody likes planning is that nobody has to do anything.
Governor Jerry Brown

• • • • MEMORY • • • •

To improve your memory, lend people money.

Writing things down is the best secret of a good memory.

The true art of memory is the art of attention.

How sweet to remember the trouble that is past!

We do not remember days, we remember moments.

We have all forgotten more than we remember.

Not the power to remember, but its very opposite, the power to forget, is a necessary condition for our existence.

How strange are the tricks of memory, which, often hazy as a dream about the most important things of a man's life, religiously preserve the merest of trifles.
Sir Richard Burton

I have a memory like an elephant.
In fact, elephants often consult me.
Noel Coward

Memory is the diary that we all carry about with us.
Oscar Wilde

• • • • MISTAKES • • • •

He who never made a mistake never made a discovery.
Samuel Smiles

Stumbling is not falling.
Portuguese proverb

The greatest mistake you can make in this life is to be
continually fearing you will make one.

*It doesn't matter how much milk you spill
so long as you don't lose your cow.*
Old Texas saying

The causes of mistakes are first, "I didn't know";
second "I didn't think"; third "I didn't care".

*No matter how desperate the predicament is, I am always
very much in earnest about clutching my cane,
straightening my derby and fixing my tie even though
I have just landed on my head.*
Charlie Chaplin

Henry Ford forgot to put a reverse gear in his first car.

*A doctor can bury his mistakes but an architect can
only advise his clients to plant vines.*
Frank Lloyd Wright

Mistakes are often the best teachers.
The shortest mistakes are always the best.
French proverb

*Any man may make a mistake;
none but a fool will persist in it.*
Latin proverb

It is very easy to forgive their mistakes.
It takes more guts and gumption to forgive them
for having witnessed your own.

*Things could be worse. Suppose your errors were counted and
published every day, like those of a baseball player.*

Wise men learn by other men's mistakes, fools by their own.

• • • • MONEY • • • •

Money talks, but it doesn't always make sense.

The only substance which can keep a cold world
from calling a citizen "Hey you!".

That element which makes stupidity shine.

The best passport.

The best tranquiliser.

The most effective labour-saving device.

The theatre's sweet music.

Money can't buy everything – poverty for example.

By the time a man has money to burn, the fire has gone out.

When money speaks the truth is silent.
Russian proverb

With money in your pocket you are wise, and you are handsome, and you sing well too.
Yiddish proverb

Money talks. It says goodbye.

If you would like to know the value of money, go and try to borrow some.

Money often costs too much.

Lack of money is the root of all evil.

It is easier to make money than to keep it.
Yiddish proverb

If only God would give me a clear sign – like making a large deposit in my name in a Swiss bank!
Woody Allen

When I had money everyone called me brother.
Polish proverb

A heavy purse makes a light heart.

If a man's after money, he's moneymad; if he keeps it he's a capitalist; if he spends it, he's a playboy. If he doesn't get it, he's a ne'er-do-well; if he doesn't try to get it, he lacks ambition. If he gets it without working for it, he's a parasite; and if he accumulates it after a lifetime of hard work people call him a fool who never got anything out of life.

A money-grabber is anyone who grabs more money than you can.

When I was young I used to think that money was the most important thing in life; now that I am old, I know it is.
Oscar Wilde

The nicest thing about money is that it never clashes with anything I wear.

I don't like money actually, but it quiets my nerves.
Joe Louis

I have enough money to last me the rest of my life, unless I buy something.

Put not your trust in money, but put your money in trust.

Some people think they are worth a lot of money because they have it.

O, what a world of vile ill-favour'd faults look handsome in three hundred pounds a year!
Shakespeare

There'll be no pockets in your shroud.

When a fellow says "It isn't the money but the principle of the thing" – it's the money.

Don't marry for money; you can borrow it cheaper.
Scottish proverb

My problem lies in reconciling my gross habits with my net income.
Errol Flynn

I'm living so far beyond my income
that we might be said to be living apart.

Saving is a very fine thing, especially if your parents
have done it for you.
Winston Churchill

Money won't buy happiness, but it will pay the salaries of a
large research staff to study the problem.

Money isn't everything; usually it isn't even enough.

All right, so I like spending money!
But name any other extravagance!
Max Kauffmann

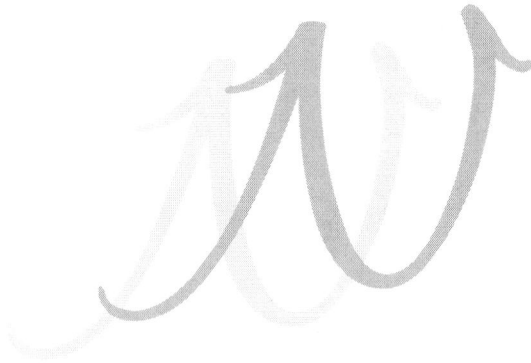

NECESSITY

Necessity makes even the timid brave.

Necessity relieves us from the embarrassment of choice.

Necessity is a hard nurse, but she raises strong children.

Necessity never made a good bargain.

Necessity turns lion into fox.
Persian proverb

Necessity, the mother of invention.

Necessity is the plea for every infringement
of human freedom. It is the argument of tyrants;
it is the creed of slaves.
William Pitt

Where necessity speaks it demands.
Russian proverb

• • • • NEGOTIATION • • • •

Don't slam the door; you might want to go back.

*When I'm getting ready to reason with a man I spend
one-third of my time thinking about myself and what
I am going to say – and two-thirds about him
and what he is going to say.*
Abraham Lincoln

A lot of times you can push someone to the wall,
and you still reach agreement, but his resentment
will come back to haunt you in a million ways.
Mark McCormack

In a successful negotiation everybody wins.

Always deal with the person who signs the cheques.

*When a man tells me he's going to put all his cards on
the table, I always look up his sleeve.*
Lord Hore-Belisha

Nothing astonishes men so much as common sense
and plain dealing.
Ralph Waldo Emerson

*My style of dealmaking is quite simple and straighforward.
I just keep pushing and pushing and pushing
to get what I'm after.*
Donald Trump

• • • • NEWS AND NEWSPAPERS • • • •

It's not the world that's got so much worse but the
news coverage that's got so much better.
GK Chesterton

*Everything you read in the newspapers is absolutely true
except for the rate story of which you happen to have
first-hand knowledge.*
Erwin Knoll

The evil that men do lives on the front pages of
greedy newspapers, but the good is often
interred apathetically inside.
Brooks Atkinson

*If some great catastrophe is not announced every morning,
we feel a certain void. "Nothing in the paper today", we sigh.*
Paul Valery

He had been kicked in the head by a mule when young,
and believed everything he read in the Sunday papers.
George Ade

*Journalism largely consists of saying 'Lord Jones Dead'
to people who never knew that Lord Jones was alive.*
GK Chesterton

An editor is one who separates the wheat
from the chaff and prints the chaff.
Adlai Stevenson

I read the newspapers avidly.
It is my one form of continuous fiction.
Aneurin Bevan

I'm with you on the free press. It's the newspapers
I can't stand.
Tom Stoppard

Four hostile newspapers are more to be feared
than a thousand bayonets.
Napoleon Bonaparte

I keep reading between the lies.
Goodman Ace

No news is good news.
Italian proverb

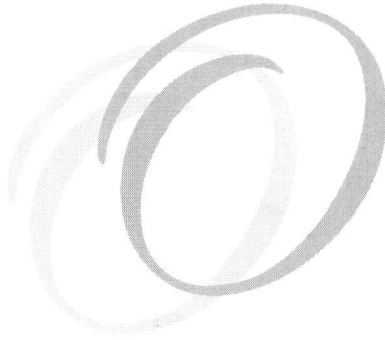

• • • • OPPORTUNITY • • • •

When the sun rises, it rises for everyone.

If opportunity doesn't knock, build a door.

Ability is nothing without opportunity.
Napoleon Bonaparte

The dawn does not come twice to awaken a man.
Arabic proverb

When writtenin Chinese the word 'crisis' is composed
of two characters. One represents danger
and the other represents opportunity.

*Small opportunities are often the beginnings
of great enterprises.*

I was seldom able to see an opportunity
until it had ceased to be one.
Mark Twain

No great man ever complains of want of opportunity.
Ralph Waldo Emmerson

Opportunity is missed by most people because
it is dressed in overalls and looks like work.
Thomas Edison

*Even when opportunity knocks, a man must get off his seat
to open the door.*

When opportunity knocks, most people
are out in the backyard looking for four-leaf clovers.

If you're looking for a big opportunity, seek out a big problem.

Not only strike while the iron is hot, but make it hot striking.
Oliver Cromwell

A wise man will make more opportunities than he finds.
Francis Bacon

There is no security on this earth; there is only opportunity.
Douglas MacArthur

• • • • OPTIMISM • • • •

*A cheerful frame of mind that enables a kettle to sing
though in hot water up to its nose.*

Keep your face to the sunshine and you cannot
see the shadow.

*In the long run the pessimist may be proved to be right,
but the optimist has a better time on the trip.*

The doctrine of belief that everything is beautiful,
including what is ugly.

*An optimist is a fellow who believes what's going to be
will be postponed.*

A mania for maintaining that all is well
when things are going badly.
Voltaire

*Optimist: a man who sets aside two hours
to do his income tax return.*

Since the house is on fire let us warm ourselves.
Italian saying

*An optimist is a man who, instead of feeling sorry that he
cannot pay his bills, is glad he is not one of his creditors.*

An optimist is someone who tells you to cheer up
when things are going his way.

• • • • PAPERWORK • • • •

Too many people are like Samuel Goldwyn, who said "I read part of it all the way through".

A memorandum is written to inform the reader
but to protect the writer.
Dean Acheson

The volume of paper expands to fill the available briefcases.
Governor Jerry Brown

If you don't know what to do with many of the papers
piled on your desk, stick a dozen colleagues' initials on them
and pass them alone. When in doubt, route.
Malcolm Forbes

• • • • PAST • • • •

It's futile to talk too much about the past – something like trying to make birth control retroactive.
Charles Edward Wilson

Nothing is more responsible for the good old days
than a bad memory.
Franklin P Adams

The golden age was never the present age.
English proverb

Every age has a keyhole to which its eye is pasted.
Mary McCarthy

The 'good old times' – all times, when old, are good.
Lord Byron

No man is rich enough to buy back the past.
Oscar Wilde

In the carriages of the past you can't go anywhere.
Maxim Gorky

Why doesn't the past decently bury itself, instead of sitting
waiting to be admired by the present.
DH Lawrence

In every age 'the good old days' were a myth.
No-one ever thought they were good at the time.
For every age has consisted of crises that seemed
intolerable to the people that lived through them.
Brooks Atkinson

History teaches us that men and nations behave wisely once
they have exhausted other alternatives.
Abba Eban

• • • • PATIENCE • • • •

A minor form of despair, disguised as virtue.

Lord grant me patience, and I want it right now.

He preacheth patience that never knew pain.

It is easy to find reasons why other folks should be patient.

Patience is bitter, but its fruit is sweet.
French proverb

Patience, the beggar's virtue.

That which in mean men we entitle patience
Is pale cold cowardice in noble breasts.
Shakespeare

Patience is the virtue of an ass, that trots beneath
its burdens, and is quiet.

Be patient; in time even an egg will walk.
African proverb

A handful of patience is worth more than a bushel of brains.
Dutch proverb

Nothing is so full of victory as patience.
Chinese proverb

Patience is a most necessary quality for business:
many a man would rather you heard his story
than granted his request.
Earl of Chesterfield

• • • • PERSEVERANCE • • • •

Many strokes overthrow the tallest oak.

Nothing in the world can take the place of persistence.
Calvin Coolidge

*Success seems to be largely a matter of hanging on
after others have let go.*

Victory belongs to the most persevering.
Napoleon Bonaparte

Diligence is the mother of good luck.

Fall seven times, stand up eight.
Japanese proverb

*The difference between perseverance and obstinacy
is that one comes from a strong will
and the other from a strong won't.*

There are no traffic jams when you go the extra mile.

• • • • PERSUASION • • • •

By persuading others, we convince ourselves.

Soft words are hard arguments.

*You can get much farther with a kind word
and a gun than a kind word alone.*
Al Capone

People are generally better persuaded by the reasons
which they have themselves discovered than by
those which come into the minds of others.
Pascal

*If you can engage people's pride, love, pity, ambition
(or whatever is their prevailing passion) on your side
you need not fear what their reason can do against you.*
Lord Chesterfield

Few are open to conviction, but the majority of men
are open to persuasion.
Goethe

• • • • PESSIMISM • • • •

Scratch a pessimist, and you find often a defender of privilege.
Lord Beveridge

Pessimism is the triumph of worry over matter.

*Pessimism is a sickness you treat like any other sickness.
The object is to get well of it as soon as possible,
and get back to business.*
Aristotle Onassis

To believe a thing impossible is to make it so.
French proverb

*Man who says it cannot be done
should not interrupt man doing it.*
Chinese proverb

Cheer up. The worst is yet to come.

• • • • A PESSIMIST IS: • • • •

One who, when he has the choice of two evils, chooses both.

A man with a difficulty for every solution.

*A person who can look at the land of milk and honey
and see only the calories and cholesterol.*

A man who financed an optimist.

*A person who, when smelling flowers,
looks around for the funeral.*

A person to borrow money from –
he never expects to be repaid.

*A pessimist is a man who thinks all women are bad.
An optimist is one who hopes they are.*

• • • • PLANNING • • • •

Make no little plans; they have no magic to stir men's blood.
Daniel Burnham

Do not plan for ventures before finishing what's at hand.

It is a bad plan that admits of no modification.

Plans get you into things but you got to work your way out.
Will Rogers

People who fail to plan, have planned to fail.

Long-range planning does not deal with future decisions,
but with the future of present decisions.
Peter Drucker

Dig a well before you are thirsty.
Chinese proverb

When schemes are laid in advance, it is surprising how often
the circumstances fit in with them.
Sir William Osler

Chance favours only the prepared mind.
Louis Pasteur

Men never plan to be failures; they simply fail
to plan to be successful.
William A Ward

• • • • POLITICS • • • •

Practical politics consists in ignoring facts.
Henry Adams

Lincoln was right, of course; you can't fool all of the people
all of the time; but you only have to fool a majority.

Politics: the gentle art of getting votes from the poor
and campaign funds from the rich, by promising
to protect each from the other.
Oscar Ameringer

*Politicians are the same all over. They promise to
build a bridge even when there is no river.*
Nikita Khrushchev

A politician is an animal that can sit on a fence
and keep both ears to the ground.
HL Mencken

*The most successful politician is he who says what
everybody is thinking most often and in a loud voice.*
Theodore Roosevelt

Being in politics is like being a football coach.
You have to be smart enough to understand the game
and stupid enough to think it's important.
Eugene McCarthy

*An honest politician is one who, when he is bought,
will stay bought.*
Simon Cameron

Probably the most distinctive characteristic of the
sucessful politician is selective cowardice.
Richard Harris

*If you want to succeed in politics, you must keep
your conscience well under control.*
David Lloyd George

Have you ever seen a candidate talking to
a rich person on television.
Art Buchwald

We all know that Prime Ministers are wedded to the truth,
but like other wedded couples they sometimes live apart.
HH Munro

There's just one rule for politicians all over the world:
don't say in power what you say in opposition.
If you do, you only have to carry out
what the other fellows have found impossible.
John Galsworthy

He knows nothing and he thinks he knows everything.
That clearly points to a political career.
George Bernard Shaw

Politics: a strife of interests masquerading as
a contest of principles.
Ambrose Bierce

• • • • POVERTY • • • •

The easiest way to remain poor is to pretend to be rich.

It is easier to praise poverty than to bear it.

I wasn't born in a log cabin, but my family
moved into one as soon as they could afford it.
Melville D Landon

Honest poverty is a gem that even a king might be
proud to call his own, but I wish to sell out.
Mark Twain

We who are liberal and progressive know that the poor are our equals in every sense except that of being equal to us.
Lionel Trilling

The trouble with being poor is that it takes up all your time.
Willem de Kooning

An empty purse frightens away friends.
Thomas Fuller

The rich would have to eat money,
but luckily the poor provide food.
Russian proverb

Empty pockets make empty heads.
William Carlos Williams

Poverty is no disgrace, but no honour either.
Yiddish proverb

*Look at me. Worked myself up from nothing
to a state of extreme poverty.*
SJ Perelman

The most inconvenient feature about poverty
is that one is apt to get used to it.

*The poor are rightfully the property of the rich,
because the rich made them.*

It is the weariness of the poor that keeps the rich in power.

*Poverty: the condition we try to conceal at the time
and then brag about it in our memoirs.*
FG Kerman

• • • • POWER • • • •

Lust of power is the strongest of all passions.
Latin proverb

*Nearly all men can stand adversity, but if you want
to test a mam's character, give him power.*
Abraham Lincoln

I'm caught in a power struggle. My boss has the power
and I have the struggle.

Power is the ability to make changes.

When I make a movie I am like God. I have the world in my
hands. I make it come out any way I want, decide who lives
and who dies, who gets funished, and who gets to live happily
ever after. In between pictures is my seventh day, I rest.
John Huston

*Those who have been once intoxicated with power, and have
derived any kind of emolument from it, even though but for
one year, can never willingly abandon it.*
Edmund Burke

A friend in power is a friend lost.
Henry Adams

The pursuit of power explains most human behaviour.
Nietzsche

Power can corrupt but absolute power
is absolutely delightful.

We thought because we had power we had wisdom.
Stephen Vincent Benet

Our sense of power is more vivid when we break a
man's spirit than when we win his heart.
Eric Hoffer

*Power, when exercised over matter or over man,
is partial to simplification.*

A cock has great influence on his own dunghill.

The eagle suffers little birds to sing.
Shakespeare

If you would be powerful, pretend to be powerful.
Horne Took

The measure of a man is what he does with power.

The reputation of power is power.
Thomas Hobbes

Even weak men when united are powerful.
Frederick Schiller

Power does not corrupt. Fear corrupts,
perhaps the fear of a loss of power.
John Steinbeck

*Power is not only what you have but what the
enemy thinks you have.*

Easy lies the head that wears a crown.
Shakespeare

Power is delightful and absolute power is absolutely delightful.
Lord Lester of Herne Hill

The most powerful people on earth are focus groups.
Bill Clinton

• • • • PRAISE AND FLATTERY • • • •

Praise undeserved is satire in disguise.

I suppose flattery hurts no-one, that is, if he doesn't inhale.
Adlai Stevenson

*What really flatters a man is that you think him
worth flattering.*
George Bernard Shaw

Some people pay a compliment as if they expected a receipt.
Kim Hubbard

*None are more apt to praise others extravagently than
those who desire to be praised themselves.*

Get someone else to blow your horn and the sound
will carry twice as far.
Will Rogers

*One catches more flies with a spoonful of honey
than with twenty casks of vinegar.*
French proverb

Flattery never comes up the expectancy of conceit.

Compliments cost nothing, yet many pay dear for them.

I didn't hear all the boss said – I was on my knees at the time.

A 'Yes man' is a guy who kisses his boss on all cheeks.

He who knows how to flatter also knows how to slander.
Napoleon Bonaparte

*Flattery is a base coin which is current only
through our vanity.*

The advantage is doing one's praising to oneself is that one
can lay it on so thick and exactly in the right places.
Samuel Butler

Praise makes good men better and bad men worse.
Thomas Fuller

Praises from an enemy imply real merit.

Thre's no praise to beat the sort you can put in your pocket.
Moliere

We begin to praise when we begin to see
a thing needs our assistance.
Thoreau

*If you can't think of any other way to flatter a man,
tell him he's the kind of man who can't be flattered.*

Flattery is the art of telling another person
exactly what he thinks of himself.

• • • • PREJUDICE • • • •

Prejudice is a great time-saver. You can form opinions without having to get the facts.

The difference between a prejudice and a conviction is that you can explain a conviction without getting mad.

We hate some persons because we do not know them; and we will not know them because we hate them.
Charles Coulton

Prejudice is the child of ignorance.
William Hazlitt

Everyone is a prisoner of his own experiences. No-one can eliminate prejudices – just recognise them.
Edward R Murrow

The tendancy of the casual mind is to pick out or stumble upon a sample which supports or defies its prejudices, and then to make it representative of a whole class.
Walter Lippmann

A prejudice is a vagrant opinion without any visible means of support.
Ambrose Bierce

He who never leaves his country is full of prejudices.
Goldoni

• • • • PRIDE • • • •

What the world needs is more geniuses with humility.
There are so few of us left.
Oscar Levant

If a proud man makes me keep my distance, the comfort
is that he keeps his at the same time.
Jonathan Swift

Every day when he looked into the glass, and gave the last
touch to his consummate toilette, he offered his grateful thanks
to Providence that his family was not unworthy of him.
Benjamin Disraeli

Pride goes before, and shame follows after.

• • • • PROVERB • • • •

Never underestimate a man who over-estimates himself.

Franklin D Roosevelt on General, Douglas MacArthur

He was like a cock who thought the sun had risen
to hear him crow.
George Elliot

Pride is the mark of one's own faults.
Hebrew proverb

The truly proud man knows neither superiors nor inferiors.
The first he does not admit of – the last he
does not concern himself about.
William Hazlitt

• • • • PROBLEMS • • • •

The measure of success is not whether you have
a tough problem to deal with, but whether it's the
same problem you had last year.

If you're not part of the solution, you're part of the problem.

A problem, well states is a problem half solved.

If the only tool you have is a hammer, you tend to see
every problem as a nail.

A problem is an opportunity in work clothes.

Problems are not stop signs, they are guidelines.

The greater the difficulty, the greater the glory.
Cicero

Work only on problems that are manifestly important and seem
to be nearly impossible to resolve. That way, you will have a
natural market for your product and no competition.
Edwin Land, founder of Polaroid

If you think the problem is bad now,
just wait until we've solved it.
Arthur Kasspe

Problems are the price of progress. Don't bring me anything but trouble. Good news weakens me.
Charles F Kettering

• • • • PROFITS • • • •

It is a socialist idea that making profits is a vice;
I consider the real vice is making losses.
Winston Churchill

A business that makes nothing but money is a poor business.
Henry Ford

When shallow critics denounce the profit motive inherent
in our system of private enterprise they ignore the fact that
it is an economic support of every human right we possess.
Without it all rights would disappear.
Dwight D Einsenhower

Watch the costs and the profits will take care of themselves.
Andrew Carnegie

The smell of profit is clean and sweet, whatever the source.
Juvenal

Profits: money that has not been wasted.

Volume times zero isn't healthy.
Lee Iacocca

*Every business has two financial objectives: one is to make
money; the other, more elusive, is to make money consistently.*

• • • • PROGRESS • • • •

The reasonable man adapts himself to the world;
the unreasonable man persists in trying to adapt the
world to himself. Therefore all progress depends on
the unreasonable man.
George Bernard Shaw

*The world is moving so fast these days that the man who says it
can't be done is generally interrupted by someone doing it.*

All progress is based upon a universal innate desire on
the part of every organism to live beyond its income.
Samuel Butler

*At every crossway on the road that leads to the future,
each progressive spirit is opposed by a thousand men
appointed to guard the past.*

All progress grows out of discontent with things as they are:
discomfort, disgust, displeasure, dissatisfaction, disease.

*In human affairs, the best stimulus for running ahead
is to have something we must run from.*

Progress imposes not only new possibilites for the future
but new restrictions.

Is it progress if a cannibal uses a knife and fork.

• • • • PROMISES • • • •

A man apt to promise is apt to forget.

Don't put it in my ear, but in my hand.
Russian proverb

He loses his thanks who promises and delays.
Latin proverb

A promise is binding in the inverse ratio
of the numbers to whom it is made.

Vows made in storms are forgot in calm.
English proverb

We promise according to our hopes,
and perform according to our fears.
La Rochefoucauld

Everyone's a millionaire where promises are concerned.

We promise much to avoid giving little.

An acre of performance is worth the whole Land of Promise.
James Howell

Half the promises people say were never kept,
were never made.
Ed Howe

He who is the most slow in making a promise
is the most faithful in the performance of it.
Rousseau

• • • • PROMOTION • • • •

If you work faithfully eight hours a day you may eventually get promoted high enough to work twelve hours a day.

You promote yourself every time you take on a new responsibility.

Comrades, you have lost a good captain to make him an ill general.
Montaigne

Mr Morgan buys his partners; I grow my own.
Andrew Carnegie

In a hierarchy, every employee tends to raise to his level of incompetence.
Laurence Peter

To blame a promotion that fails on the promoted person, as is usually done, is no more rational than to blame a capital investment that has gone sour on the money that was put into it.
Peter Drucker

I made myself almost too good as Number Two. So, in effect, what I had to do to get promoted was to get my boss promoted. Which I would advise anyone to do. That may sound cynical, but if you want to get ahead, promote your boss.
William George

• • • • PROPERTY • • • •

An acre in Middlesex is better than a principality in Utopia.
Macaulay

*Thieves respect property. They merely wish the property to
become their property that they may more perfectly respect it.*
GK Chesterton

When the white man came, we had the land and they had
the Bibles. Now they have the land and we have the Bibles.
Chief Dan George

*Property is the fruit of labour; property is desirable; it is a
positive good in the world. That someone should be rich shows
that others may become rich, and hence, is just another
encouragement to industry and enterprise.*
Abraham Lincoln

Property: a bleach that takes stains out of character.

*Our houses are such unwieldy property that we are often
imprisoned rather than housed in them.*
Thoreau

The dog is a lion in his own house.
Persian proverb

• • • • PRUDENCE • • • •

Prudence is a rich, ugly old maid courted by incapacity.
William Blake

Call the bear 'Uncle' till you are safe across the bridge.
Turkish proverb

No wise man stands behind an ass when he kicks.

A prudent man does not make the goat his gardener.
Hungarian proverb

He who wants a rose must respect the thorn.
Persian proverb

Measure a thousand times and cut once.
Turkish proverb

Caution, though often wasted, is a good risk to take.
Josh Billings

Caution is the eldest child of wisdom.
Victor Hugo

*Drink nothing without seeing it, sign nothing
without reading it.*
Spanish proverb

Get out of the forest while you still have daylight.
Japanese proverb

• • • • PUBLISHING • • • •

*There is some kind of notion abroad that because a book is
humorous the publisher has to be funnier and madder than
hell in marketing it.*
SJ Perelman

No author is a man of genius to his publisher.
Heinrich Heine

*All a publisher has to do is write cheques at intervals,
while a lot of deserving and industrious chappies
rally round and do the real work.*
PG Wodehouse

The relationship of an agent to a publisher
is that of a knife to a throat.
Marvin Josephson

*You cannot or at least should not try to argue with authors.
Too many are like children whose tears can suddenly be
changed to smiles if they are handled the right way.*
Michael Joseph, publisher

After being turned down by numerous publishers
he decided to write for posterity.
George Ade

Aren't we due a royalty statement?
Prince Charles to his literary agent

ˌ• • • • PUNCTUALITY • • • •

Punctuality is something that, if you have it,
there's often no-one around to share it with you.

Punctuality is the virtue of the bored.

I've been on a calendar, but never on time.
Marilyn Monroe

Punctuality: the art of guessing correctly how late the other party is going to be.

Punctuality is the politeness of kings.
King Louis XVIII of France

Some people are always late, like the late King George V.
Spike Milligan

Men count up the faults of those who keep them waiting.
French proverb

The trouble with being punctual is that people think you have nothing more important to do.

If you're there before it's over, you're on time.
James Walker

• • • • QUALITY • • • •

Quality is not an act. It is a habit.
Aristotle

Quality in a service or product is not what you put into it.
It is what the client or customer gets out of it.
Peter Drucker

Quality is never an accident; it is always the result
of intelligent effort.
John Ruskin

Conceal a flaw, and the world will imagine the worst.

Good quality is cheap; it's poor quality that is expensive.
Joe L Griffith

• • • • QUESTIONS • • • •

The 'silly question' is the first intimation
of some totally new development.

The uncreative mind can spot wrong answers,
but it takes a creative mind to spot wrong questions.

He who asks is a fool for five minutes,
but he who does not ask remains a fool forever.
Chinese proverb

Judge a man by his questions rather than by his answers.
Voltaire

Millions saw the apple fall but Newton was
the one to ask why.

Better ask twice than lose your way once.
Danish proverb

To question a wise man is the beginning of wisdom.
German proverb

There aren't any embarrassing questions –
just embarrassing answers.

• • • • REASON • • • •

Nothing has an uglier look to us than reason,
when it is not on our side.

*A man always has two reasons for doing anything –
a good reason and the real reason.*
JP Morgan

The man who listens to reason is lost: reason enslaves all
those whose minds are not strong enough to master her.
George Bernard Shaw

*We may take fancy for a companion,
but follow reason as our guide.*

Samuel Johnson

The last function of reason is to recognise that
there are an infinity of things which surpass it.
Pascal

*It is useless for us to attempt to reason a man out of
a thing he has never been reasoned into.*
Jonathan Swift

Error of opinion may ber tolerated where reason
is left free to combat it.
Thomas Jefferson

• • • • REPUTATION • • • •

*Many a man's reputation would not know his character
if they met on the street.*
Elbert Hubbard

Do not worry about what people are thinking about you –
for they are not thinking about you. They are wondering
what you are thinking about them.

*Reputation, reputation. O, I have lost my reputation.
I have lost the immortal part, Sir, of myself
and what remains is bestial.*
Shakespeare

The only time you realise you have a reputation
is when you're not living up to it.
Jose Iturbi

It is easier to add to a good reputation than to get it.

Shall I be remembered after death? I sometimes think and
hope so. But I trust I may not be found out before my death.
Samuel Butler

Reputation is often got without merit and lost without fault.
English proverb

How many 'coming men' has one known!
Where on earth do they all go to?
Sir Arthur Pinero

• • • • RESEARCH • • • •

*Research is to see what everybody else has seen,
and to think what nobody else has thought.*

Research is an organised method of keeping you
reasonably dissatisfied with what you have.
Charles Kettering

*The outcome of any serious research can only be to make
two questions grow where only one grew before.*
Thorstein Veblen

Basic research is when I'm doing what
I don't know I'm doing.
Werner von Braun

*Researchers have already cast much darkness on this subject
and if they continue their investigations we shall soon know
nothing at all about it.*
Mark Twain

The true worth of a researcher lies in pursuing what he did
not seek in his experiment as well as what he thought.
Claude Bernard

• • • • RESPONSIBILITY • • • •

Every man must carry his own sack to the mill.
Italian proverb

Everybody's business is nobody's business.

Responsibility is the price of greatness.
Winston Churchill

You can't escape the responsibility of tomorrow
by evading it today.
Abraham Lincoln

*That which is common to the greatest number
has the least care bestowed upon it.*
Aristotle

Unto whomsoever much is given,
of him much shall be required.
Bible

No snowflake in an avalanche ever feels responsible.

A decision is what a man makes when
he can't get anybody to serve on a committee.

*Responsibility: a detachable burden easily shifted to the
shoulders of God, Fate, Fortune, Luck or one's neighbour. In the
days of astrology it was customary to unload it upon a star.*
Ambrose Bierce

The most anxious man in prison is the governor.
George Bernard Shaw

It is easy to dodge our responsibilities but we cannot dodge the consequence of our responsibilities.
Lord Stamp

• • • • RETIREMENT • • • •

When a man retires and time is no longer a matter of urgent importance, his colleagues generally present him with a watch.
RC Sherriff

The problem with retirement is that you never know what day it is, what time it is, where you're supposed to be, or what you're supposed to be doing.
It's a lot like working for the government.

Few men of action have been able to make a graceful exit at the appropriate time.
Malcolm Muggeridge

Two weeks is about the ideal length of time to retire.
Alex Comfort

The best time to start thinking about your retirement is before the boss does.

Retirement kills more people than hard work ever did.
Malcolm Forbes

When a man retires, his wife gets twice the husband but only half the income.

Retirement from the concert world is like giving up smoking.
You have got to finish completely.
Beniamino Gigli

Americans hardly ever retire from business: they are either
carried out feet first or they jump from a window.
AL Goodheart

When you retire from the company you have to
turn in your ulcers.

• • • • REVENGE • • • •

Revenge is a confession of pain.
Latin proverb

Revenge is a dish that should be eaten cold.
English proverb

In taking revenge, a man is but even with his enemy;
but in passing it over, he is superior.
Francis Bacon

Revenge is a luscious fruit which you must leave to ripen.

Blood cannot be washed out with blood.
Persian proverb

Living well is the best revenge.

Nothing is more costly, nothing is more sterile,
than vengeance.
Winston Churchill

Revenge is often like biting a dog because the dog bit you.

A man that studieth revenge keeps his own wounds green.
Francis Bacon

Heat not a furnace for your foe so hot
that it do singe thyself.
Shakespeare

• • • • RISK • • • •

A ship in harbour is safe, but that is not what
ships are built for.

Behold the turtle. He makes progress only
when he sticks his neck out.

Safe is risky.

Take calculated risks.
That is quite different from being rash.
George S Patton

What would you attempt in life
if you knew you could not fail.

Why not go out on a limb. Isn't that where the fruit is?

The desire for safety stands against
every great and noble enterprise.
Tacitus

• • • • RULES • • • •

Hell, there are no rules here –
we're trying to accomplish something.
Thomas Edison

Rules are for when brains run out.

Golden rule: he who has the gold makes the rules.

The golden rule is that there are no golden rules.

••••• SCIENCE •••••

The whole of science is nothing more than a refinement of everyday thinking.
Einstein

There is something fascinating about science.
One gets such wholesale returns of conjecture
out of such a trifling investment of fact.
George Bernard Shaw

*Basic research is what I am doing when
I don't know what I'm doing.*
Werner von Braun

My greatest discovery of all was the discovery of
what people want to use.
Thomas Edison

*In science the credit goes to the man who convinces
the world, not to the man to whom the idea first occurs.*
William Osler

Science has always promised two things not necessarily related – an increase first in our powers, second in our happiness and wisdom, and we have come to realise that it is the first and less important of the two promises which it has kept most abundantly.
Joseph Wood Krutch

The true scientist never loses the faculty of amazement.
It is the essence of his being.
Hans Selye

A drug is a substance that when injected into a guinea pig produces a scientific paper.

Science should be on tap, not on top.
Winston Churchill

The science of today is the technology of tomorrow.

When I find myself in the company of scientists,
I feel like a shabby curate who has strayed into
a drawing room full of dukes.
WH Auden

This is the essence of science: ask an impertinent question, and you are on your way to a pertinent answer.
Jacob Bronowski

Science is a first-rate piece of furniture for a man's upper
chamber if he has common sense on the ground floor.
Oliver Wendell Holmes

If it squirms, it's biology; if it stinks, it's chemistry,
if it doesn't work, it's physics and if you can't
understand it, it's mathematics.
Magnus Pike

• • • • SECRETS • • • •

*There are some occasions when a man must tell
half his secret in order to conceal the rest.*

A secret is something that is not only told in strict
confidence, but also repeated in strict confidence.

*Most of us can keep a secret –
it's the people we tell it to that can't.*

You do people a good turn when you trust them with
a secret: they feel so important while telling it.

*The vanity of being known to be trusted with a secret
is generally one of the chief motives to disclose it.*

A company for carrying on an undertaking of
Great Advantage but no-one to know what it is.
(Company prospects at the time of the South Sea Bubble).

The best leaks always take place in the urinal.
John Cole (journalist)

Nothing is so burdensome as a secret.
French proverb

Many a secret that cannot be pried out by curiosity
can be drawn out by indifference.
Sydney J Harris

• • • • SECURITY • • • •

The man who looks for security, even in the mind,
is like a man who would chop off his limbs in order to have
artificial ones which will give him no pain or trouble.
Henry Miller

The most beaten paths are certainly the surest;
but do not hope to scare up much game on them.
Andre Gide

Some of the most insecure things in the world
are called 'securities'.

The protected man doesn't need luck;
therefore it seldom visits him.
Alan Harrington

People wish to be settled; only as far as they are
unsettled is there any hope for them.
Ralph Waldo Emerson

The physic task which a person can and must do
for himself is not to feel secure
but to be able to tolerate insecurity.
Erich Fromm

• • • • SELLING • • • •

Sell the sizzle, not the steak.

A man without a smiling face must not open a shop.
Chinese proverb

Sales resistance is the triumph of mind over patter.

If you want to buy from us we speak English,
but if you want to sell to us you must speak German.
Helmut Kohl

Don't oversell. If you do, it's like knocking on a
turtle shell trying to get him to stick his head out.

Don't sell me books, sell me knowledge.

Don't sell me insurance, sell me peace of mind
and a secure future for my family.
Don't sell me clothes, sell me style, attractiveness
and a sharper image. Don't sell me a house,
sell me comfort and pride in ownership.

Who will sell a blind horse praises the feet.
German proverb

The fish sees the bait, not the hook.
Chinese proverb

"Don't you know that you can't sell insurance
without a licence?"
"I knew I wasn't selling any but I didn't know the reason."

He's a very independent salesman –
he takes orders from nobody.

*An ideal salesman has the curiosity of a cat, the tenacity
of a bulldog, the friendship of a little child, the diplomacy
of a wayward husband, the patience of a self-sacrificing wife,
the enthusiasm of a Sinatra fan, the assurance of a
Harvard man, the good humour of a comedian, the simplicity
of a jackass, and the tireless energy of a bill collector.*
Harry G Moock

I stand behind every car I sell. I help push it.

*The sales manager stood before the progress chart which
indicated the sales of each representative with coloured pins.
"Smith", he said, "I'm not going to fire you,
but just to emphasise the insecurity of your position
I'm loosening the pin a little."*

To salesman: a live wire with good connections.

*First salesman: "I made some very valuable contacts today".
Second salesman: "I didn't get any orders either".*

I used to sell furniture for a living.
The trouble was it was my own.
Les Dawson

*Auctioneer: a man who proclaims with a hammer
that he has picked a pocket with his tongue.*
Ambrose Bierce

• • • • SEX • • • •

If it wasn't for pickpockets and frisking at airports
I wouldn't have any sex life at all.
Rodney Dangerfield

*A man who marries his mistress creates a vacancy
in the position.*
James Goldsmith

It's so long since I've had sex I've forgotten
who ties up whom.
Joan Rivers

*Ten men waiting for me at the door?
Send one of them home, I'm tired.*
Mae West

Basically, I wanted a woman who was an economist in the
kitchen and a whore in bed. I wound up with a woman who
was a whote in the kitchen and an economist in bed.
Geoffrey Gorer

What part of 'no' don't you understand.
Rita Rudner

Sex - the poor man's polo.

*A promiscuous person is someone who
is getting more sex than you are.*
Victor Lownes

I'm such a good lover because I practise a lot on my own.
Woody Allen

Man cannot live by bed alone.

I don't see so much of Alfred any more
since he got so interested in sex.
Mrs Alfred Kinsey

*It doesn't matter what you do in the bedroom as long as you
don't do it in the streets and frighten the horses.*
Mrs Patrick Campbell

He said it was artificial respiration, but now I find
that I am to have his child.

I am always looking for meaningful one-night stands.
Dudley Moore

• • • • SILENCE • • • •

Keep quiet and people will think you are a philosopher.
Latin proverb

Silence is the most perfect expression of scorn.
George Bernard Shaw

Silence is one of the hardest arguments to refute.
GK Chesterton

*Better to remain silent and be thought a fool,
than to speak out and remove all doubt.*
Abraham Lincoln

Silence is also speech.
Yiddish proverb

The silent dog is the first to bite.
German proverb

In human intercourse the tragedy begins,
not when there is misunderstanding about words,
but when silence is not understood.
Thoreau

That man's silence is wonderful to listen to.
Thomas Hardy

The most silent people are generally those
who think most highly of themselves.
William Hazlitt

Most of us know how to say nothing. Few of us know when.

A man is known by the silence he keeps.

• • • • SIMPLICITY • • • •

Less is more.
Robert Browning

The ability to simplify means to eliminate the
unnecessary so that the necessary may speak.
Hans Hoffmann

Simplicity is the mean between ostentation and rusticity.
Alexander Pope

Affected simplicity is an elegant imposture.
La Rochefoucauld

*It is proof of high culture to say the greatest
matters in the simplest way.*
Ralph Waldo Emerson

Simplicity is the most deceitful mistress
that ever betrayed man.
Henry Adams

*Simplicity of character is the natural result
of profound thought.*
William Hazlitt

He was a simple soul who had not been introduced
to his own subconscious.
Warwick Deeping

• • • • SINCERITY • • • •

People are always sincere. They change sincerities that's all.
Tristan Bernard

I am not sincere, even when I am saying that
I am not sincere.
Jules Renard

It's never what you say, but how you make it sound sincere.
Marya Mannes

A little sincerity is a dangerous thing
and a great deal of it is absolutely fatal.
Oscar Wilde

Weak people cannot be sincere.
La Rochefoucauld

To stupid people sincerity is one continuous
process of self-sacrifice.

*The most exhausting thing in life, I have discovered,
is being insincere.*
Anne Morrow Lindbergh

• • • • SIZE • • • •

Size isn't everything. The whale is endangered,
while the ant continues to do just fine.
Bill Vaughan

*If you think you're too small to have an impact,
try going to bed with a mosquito in your room.*
Anita Roddick

Great engines turn on small pivots.
English proverb

*Any intelligent fool can make things bigger, more complex,
and more violent. It takes a touch of genius – and a lot
of courage – to move in the opposite direction.*
EF Schumacher

If you can build a business up big enough, it's respectable.
Will Rogers

The dinosaur's eloquent lesson is that if some bigness is good,
an overbundance of bigness is not necessarily better.
Eric Johnston

A big corporation is more or less blamed for being big;
it is only big if it gives service. If it doesn't give service,
it gets small faster than it grew big.
William Knudsen

• • • • SLANDER • • • •

A slander is like a hornet; if you cannot kill it dead
the first blow, better not strike at it.
HW Shaw

If slander be a snake, it is a winged one –
it flies as well as creeps.
Douglas Jerrold

People are more slanderous from vanity than from malice.
La Rochefoucauld

Folk whose own behaviour is most ridiculous
are always to the fore in slandering others.
Moliere

Slander, like coal, will either dirty your hand or burn it.
Russian proverb

The more implausible a slander is,
the better fools remember it.

It takes your enemy and your friend, working together,
to hurt you to the heart; the one to slander you
and the other to get the news to you.
Mark Twain

Have patience awhile; slanders are not long-lived.
Truth is the child of time; ere long she shall appear
to vindicate thee.
Immanuel Kant

• • • • SLEEP • • • •

The amount of sleep required by the average person
is just five minutes more.

A man is not always asleep when his eyes are shut.

Sleeping at the wheel is a good way to keep from growing old.

Sleep is the best cure for waking troubles.
Spanish proverb

Sleep: the poor man's wealth.

Laugh and the world laughs with you,
snore and you sleep alone.
Anthony Burgess

That we are not much sicker and much madder
than we are is due exclusively to that most blessed
and blessing of all natural graces, sleep.
Aldous Huxley

The best thing about lying in bed late is that
you learn to distinguish between first things and trivia,
for whatever presses on you has to prove its importance
before it makes you move.
Max Lerner

There will be sleeping enough in the grave.

• • • • SMOKING • • • •

As ye smoke, so shall ye reek.

Tobacco: the Indian's revenge.

The best cigarette filter is the cellophane
on an unwrapped package.

*I kissed my first woman and smoked my first cigarette
on the same day; I have never had time for tobacco since.*
Arturo Toscanini

To the average smoker the world is his ashtray.
Alexander Chase

*I have every sympathy with the American who was
so horrified by what he had read about the
effects of smoking that he gave up reading.*
Henry G Strauss

Perfection is such a nuisance that I often regret
having cured myself of using tobacco.
Emile Zola

Smoking is very bad for you and should only be done because it looks so good. People who don't smoke have a terrible time finding something polite to do with their lips.
PJ O'Rourke

• • • • SNOBBERY • • • •

A fine imitation of self-esteem for those
who can't afford the real thing.
Frederick Morton

Laughter would be bereaved if snobbery died.
Peter Ustinov

Yeats is becoming so aristocratic,
he's evicting imaginary tenants.
Oliver St John Gogarty

The true snob never rests; there is always a higher goal to attain, and there are, by the same token, always more and more people to look down upon.
Russell Lynes

All think their little set mankind.
Hannah More

An uppish class sometimes mistakes itself for an upper class.

Snobbery is the pride of those who are not sure
of their position.

The superiority of some men is merely local.
They are great because their associates are little.
Samuel Johnson

Snobs talk as if they had begotten their own ancestors.
Herbert Agar

• • • • SPEAKING • • • •

There is all the difference in the world between having
something to say and having to say something.

The public speaker who drives home too many facts
will drive home too many listeners.

Always be shorter than anyone dared hope.

After-dinner speeches would be much shorter
if they were given before dinner.

An impromtu speech is seldom worth
the paper it is written on.

I do not object to people looking at their watches
when I am speaking, but I strongly object when they start
shaking them to make certain they are still going.
Lord Birkett

An after dinner speech should be like a lady's dress: long
enough to cover the subject but short enough to be interesting.

Public speaking is like drinking: knowing how to start is less
important than knowing when to stop.

*The surest way to stay awake during an
after-dinner speech is to deliver it.*

Many a public speaker begins with not knowing what he is
going to say and ends with not knowing what he has said.

*The hardest thing about making a speech
is knowing what to do with your hands.*

• • • • SPEECH (Opening) • • • •

Thank you for the generous introduction.
After that I can hardly wait to hear what I have to say.

*Coming here today, my wife offered me some sage advice.
"Don't try to be charming, witty, or intellectual.
Just be yourself."*

Sometimes I feel like Graucho Marx, who said:
"Before I speak I have something important to say".

*I hope that when I've finished speaking, I don't experience
what Adlai Stevenson did the time he spoke at a small college.
When the speech was over, a young man approached him
and said: "Mr Stevenson, that was a wonderful speech –
absolutely superfluous". Stevenson was taken aback
but graciously replied: "Thank you. I'm glad you liked it.
I intend to have it published posthumously."
The student replied: "Great. The sooner the better".*

The last time our chairman introduced me and was told to be
brief, he began "The less said about William Davis, the better..."

Speaking to you today, I'm violating one of the three pieces or immortal advice from Winston Churchill, who said: "Never try to walk up a wall that's leaning towards you. Never try to kiss a person that's leaning away from you. And never speak to a group that knows more about the subject than you do".

A toastmaster once advised me that an after-dinner speech should always be short.
He said: Be accurate! Be brief! And then be seated.

Ladies and gentlemen, I promise you that I shall be as brief as possible – no matter how long it takes me.

Thank you for that marvellous obituary.

I'm so confident tonight, I didn't even wear my best suit.

I once heard a chairman say: Mr Jones will now give his address. Mr Jones got up and said: 339 Park Avenue. And sat down again.

Your chairman just said to me: "Would you like to speak now or shall we let them go on enjoying themselves for a little longer?".

At your reception earlier someone said to me: "Oh I have heard so much about you, now I'd like to hear your side of the story".

For those of you who have had a heavy day I've booked an alarm call for the end of my speech.

Your chairman asked if I believed in free speech.
I said of course I did – it's fundamental to our democracy.
He said "Good, can you make one next week?".

Friends. Well I feel I know you too well
to call you ladies and gentlemen.

I'm sorry I am late. The lift said 'Six people only'.
So I had to wait for five more.

I'm the only one on the top table I have never heard of.

It's a change to find my name in bigger type than the soup.

I'm not a proud speaker. If you don't wish to applaud
I'll settle for enthusiastic nods.

You will be relieved to hear that I do not intend
to use the full two hours allotted to me.

• • • • SPEECH (Heckle Stoppers) • • • •

I shall have to ask your mother to take you home.

Any more cracks like that and your wife and I are through.

I'd like to help you out – tell me,
which way did you come in?

What exactly is on your mind?
If you'll excuse the exaggeration.

If I want you, I'll rattle your cage.

Were you there for the fitting of that suit.

You seem happy tonight. No school tomorrow?

Must be a full moon tonight.

He must be a bundle of fun at home.

• • • • SPEECH (Closers) • • • •

Since I have always believed that speeches should end
on the same day they begin – I'll close now.

*I'm going to end before I end up like the medieval knight
who returned home to his castle in very poor shape.
He was bruised and battered. His armour was dented
in a dozen places, and he was practically falling off his horse.
When the king came out to greet him, he asked the knight
what on earth had happened.
The knight said: "My lord, I merely went out to talk
to your enemies in the west".
The king said: "But I don't have any enemies in the west".
The knight said: "Well, now you do!"*

I am going to sit down before I make any more enemies.

• • • • STUPIDITY • • • •

*When a finger points at the moon,
the imbecile looks at the finger.*
Chinese proverb

He that hath a head of wax must not walk in the sun.
English proverb

He that makes himself an ass
must not take it ill if men ride him.
Thomas Fuller

It is so pleasant to come across people more stupid
than ourselves. We love them at once for being so.
Jerome K Jerome

Whenever a man does a stupid thing
it is always from the noblest motive.
Oscar Wilde

Better an empty purse than an empty head.
German proverb

Nothing in all the world is more dangerous than sincere
ignorance and conscientious stupidity.
Martin Luther King Jr

What makes stupidity really insufferable is that it is
forever in action – ignorance knows no rest.

• • • • STYLE • • • •

Style is when they're running you out of town and you
make it look like you're leading the parade.
William Battie

Style is a magic wand, and turns everything to gold
that it touches.
Logan Pearsall Smith

*In matters of grave important, style, not sincerity,
is the vital thing.*
Oscar Wilde

The only real elegance is in the mind; if you've got that,
the rest really comes from it.
Diana Vreeland

Style is the dress of thoughts.
Lord Chesterfield

• • • • SUCCESS • • • •

To succeed, jump as quickly at opportunities
as you do at conclusions.
Benjamin Franklin

*For every person who climbs the ladder of success
there are a dozen waiting for the elevator.*

Success is a great deodorant.

*Secrets for succes: 1. Get up early. 2. Work hard.
3. Strike oil.*

Eighty per cent of success is showing up.
Woody Allen

Success is a journey, not a destination.

Everybody loves success, but they hate successful people.
John McEnroe

*Success gives some people big heads
and others big headaches.*

Success has many friends.
Greek proverb

*A successful man is one who makes more money
than his wife can spend. A successful woman
is one who can find such a man.*
Lana Turner

Success as ruined many a man.
Benjamin Franklin

*Every man who is high up loves to think that he has done
it all himself; and the wife smiles and lets it go at that.*
JM Barrie

The common idea that success spoils people
by making them vain, egotistic, and self-complacent
is erroneous; on the contrary, it makes them,
for the most part, humble, tolerant and kind.
Failure makes people cruel and bitter.
Somerset Maugham

*There is always something about success
that displeases even your best friends.*
Oscar Wilde

All you need in this life is ignorance and confidence,
and then success is sure.

Mark Twain

*Success is the ability to get along with some people
and ahead of others.*

Successful people are the ones who can think up
things for the rest of the world to keep busy at.

*One of the great advantages of success lies in the fact
that you don't have to listen to good advice any more.*

Success: when a man stops keeping track of
the money and starts counting calories.

*The only place where success comes before work
is in the dictionary.*

The penalty of success is to be bored by the people
who used to snub you.

Nancy Astor

*There is no secret about success. Did you ever know
a successful man that didn't tell you about it?*

The toughest thing about success is that you've got to keep
on being a success. Talent is only a starting point in business.
You've got to keep working that talent.

Irving Berlin

My rise to the top was through sheer ability – and inheritance.

Malcolm Forbes

The compensation of a very early success is a
conviction that life is a romantic matter.

In the best sense one stays young.
F Scott Fitzgerald

Unless a man has been taught what to do with success after getting it, the achievement of it must inevitably leave him prey to boredom.
Bertrand Russell

I should never have made my success in life
if I had not bestowed upon the least thing
I have ever undertaken the same attention and care
that I have bestowed upon the greatest.
Charles Dickens

If at first you don't succeed, redefine success.

Success is never final.
Winston Churchill

• • • • TALK • • • •

Don't talk about yourself; it will be done when you leave.

Addison Mitzner

Talk is cheap.
English proverb

The secret of being tiresome is in telling everything.
Voltaire

Some people would say more if they talked less.

I don't like people to talk while I'm interrupting.

Another of life's problems is how to keep
ignorant people from talking.

*Some people talk simply becauser they think sound
is more manageable than silence.*

The voice is a second face.

Little said is soon amended.
Cervantes

Talk does not cook rice.
Chinese proverb

People do not seem to talk for the sake of expressing their opinions, but to maintain an opinion for the sake of talking.
William Hazlitt

Many people would be more truthful if it were not for their uncontrollable desire to talk.
Edgar Watson Howe

The tongue is more to be feared than the sword.
Japanese proverb

We talk little when vanity does not make us.
La Rochefoucauld

What is uttered is finished and done with.
Thomas Mann

The unluckiest insolvent in the world is the man whose expenditure for speech is too great for his income of ideas.
Christopher Morley

They always talk who never think.
Matthew Prior

No man would listen to you talk if he didn't know it was his turn next.
Edgar Watson Howe

At a dinner party one should eat wisely
but not too well, and talk well but not too wisely.
Somerset Maugham

How time flies when you are doing all the talking.

• • • • TAXES • • • •

Everybody should pay his income tax with a smile.
I tried it, but they wanted cash.

Next to being shot at and missed, there is nothing
quite as satisfying as a tax refund.

Taxes are the way the government has of artificially
inducing the rainy day everybody has been saving for.

Taxation is the art of so plucking the goose as to
obtain the largest amount of feathers
with the least amount of hissing.

A government which robs Peter to pay Paul
can always rely on the support of Paul.
George Bernard Shaw

This is the seaon of the year when we discover that
we owe most of our success to Uncle Sam!
Wall Street Journal

It is the part of a good shepherd to fleece his flock,
not to flay it.
Tiberius

A toast to the Inland Revenue.
You really have to hand it to those boys.

*Inland Revenue: the world's most successful
mail order business.*

The taxpayer – that's someone who works for the federal
government but doesn't have to take a civil service exam.
Ronald Regan

*Income tax has made more liars out of the
American people than golf.*
Will Rogers

Income tax returns are the most imaginative
fiction being written today.
Herman Wouk

*Don't get too excited about a tax cut.
It's like a mugger giving you back fare for a taxi.*

All money nowadays seems to be produced with
a natural homing instinct for the Treasury.

*There is one difference between a tax collector and
a taxidermist – the taxidermist leaves the hide.*

The point to remember is that what the government
gives it must first take away.

• • • • TEAMWORK • • • •

No member of a crew is praised for the rugged individuality of his rowing.
Ralph Waldo Emerson

It takes two wings for a bird to fly.

It is better to have one person working with you than having three people working for you.
Dwight D Eisenhower

As the mouse said to the elephant as they walked across a bridge "together we're shaking this thing".

A single arrow is easily broken, but not ten in a bundle.
Japanese proverb

• • • • THRIFT • • • •

It is very well to be thrifty, but don't amass a hoard of regrets.

A penny saved is a penny earned.

A penny saved is a penny to squander.

Ambrose Bierce

A man often pays dear for a small frugality.
Ralph Waldo Emerson

Anyone who lives within his means suffers
from a lack of imagination.
Lionel Stander

Save water, shower with a friend.
Slogan in the 1970's

He that considers in prosperity will be
less afflicted in adversity.

Economy is too late at the bottom of the purse.

There is no profit in going to bed early
to save candles if the result is twins.

*The secret is to live as cheaply the first few days after
payday as you lived the last few days before.*

The petty economies of the rich are just as amazing
as the silly extravagances of the poor.
William Feather

• • • • TIME • • • •

*People who make the worst use of their time are the same
ones who complain that there is never enough time.*

Time is money, especially overtime.

*You can't make footprints in the sands of time
by sitting down.*

Time gives good advice.
Maltese proverb

Time is the most valuable thing a man can spend.

Until you value yourself you will not value time. Until you value your time, you will not do anything with it.

You will never find time for anything.
If you want time you must make it.

A man who has taken your time recognises no debt;
yet it is the one he can never repay.
Seneca

Counting time is not so important as making time count.

Time and tide wait for no man.
English proverb

Better late than never.

Time is money, and many people pay their debts with it.

Time is a dressmaker specialising in alterations.

Time and I against any two.
Spanish proverb

Why kill time when you can employ it?

Time wounds all heels.

I haven't the time to take my time.

Time makes more converts than reason.

Time, which changes people, does not alter
the imagine we have retained of them.
Marcel Proust

• • • • TOASTS • • • •

May you live as long as you want, and not
want as long as you live.

May the Lord love us but not call us too soon.

Let us toast the fools. But for them
the rest of us could not succeed.
Mark Twain

Love to one, friendship to many, and goodwill to all.

May we be happy and our enemies know it.

May you have warmth in your igloo, oil in your lamp,
and peace in your heart.
Eskimo toast

May the roof above us never fall in, and may
we friends gathered below never fall out.

May your fire never go out.

May your well never run dry.

Here's to becoming top banana without
losing touch with the bunch.
Bill Copeland, on a promotion

May friendship, like wine, improve as time advances, and may
we always have old wines, old friends, and young cares.

When there's snow on the roof, there's fire in the furnace.
Toast to maturity

To the Great Unknown – who is waiting to do us a favour.

May you live to a hundred years
with one extra year to repent.

A health to you,
A wealth to you,
And the best that life can give to you.
May fortune still be kind to you.
And happiness be true to you,
And life be long and good to you.
Is the toast of all your friends to you.

Here's to Eternity – may we spend it in as good company
as this night finds us.

To your good health, old friend, may you live for a
thousand years, and I be there to count them.

• • • • TRAVEL • • • •

Flying first class is a bit like being in a hospital –
they wake you up every few hours to give you orange juice.

The hotel was so up-market that even room service
was ex-directory.

There are two classes of travel – first class, and with children.
Robert Benchley

It is easier to find a travel companion
than to get rid of one.
Art Buchwald

*To give you an idea of how fast we travelled:
we left Spokane with two rabbits and when we got
to Topeka, we still only had two.*
Bob Hope

They say travel broadens the mind;
but you must have the mind.

GK Chesterton

At my age travel broadens the behind.
Stephen Fry

Always choose the oldest customs official.
No chance of promotion.
Somerset Maugham

Travel teaches toleration.
Disraeli

Fly first class – or your heirs will.

The heaviest baggage for a traveller is an empty purse.
English proverb

Hawaii has the same weather all year round.
Wonder how their conversations start?

Everybody in fifteenth-century Spain was wrong
about where China was and as a result,
Columbus discovered Caribbean vacations.
PJ O'Rourke

On a Polar expedition begin with a clear idea which Pole you
are aiming at, and try to start facing the right way. Choose
your companions carefully – you may have to eat them.
WC Sellar

Every year it takes less time to fly across the Atlantic
and more time to drive to the office.

Drive carefully! Remember it's not only a car
that can be recalled by its maker.

Like all great travellers, I have seen more than I remember,
and remember more than I have seen.
Disraeli

It used to be a good hotel, but that proves nothing –
I used to be a good boy.
Mark Twain

• • • • TROUBLE • • • •

Why hoard your troubles? They have no market value, so just
throw them away.

Never trouble trouble till trouble troubles you.

*The best place to put your troubles is in your pocket –
the one with a hole in it.*

He that seeks trouble always finds it.
English proverb

*I am an old man and have known a great many troubles,
but most of them never happened.*

Problems are the price of progress. Don't bring me
anything but trouble. Progress weakens me.

*Trouble is the structural steel that goes into
the building of character.*

Golf without bunkers and hazards would be tame
and monotonous. So would life.

A problem well stated is a problem half solved.

The greater the difficulty, the greater the glory.
Cicero

Problems are not stop signs, they are guidelines.

The trouble with trouble is that it always starts out like fun.

The way out of trouble is never as simple as the way in.

When you tell people your troubles, half of them
are not interested, and the other half are glad
to learn that you're getting what you deserve.

*The easiest way to get into trouble is to be right
at the wrong time.*

If you want to get rid of trouble it shouldn't be difficult.
There are lots of people who are always looking for it.

Nothing lasts forever – not even your troubles.

• • • • TRUST • • • •

It goes a long way towards making someone
trustworthy if you trust them.
Seneca

Trust in Allah, but tie up your camel.
Arabian proverb

To be trusted is a far greater compliment than to be loved.
Ramsay Macdonald

I never trust a man until I've got his pecker in my pocket.
Lyndon Johnson

He trusted neither of them as far as he could spit,
and he was a poor spitter,
lacking both distance and control.
PG Wodehouse

*Trust men and they will be true to you; treat them greatly
and they will show themselves great.*
Emerson

No man ever quite believes in any other man.
One may believe in an idea absolutely, but not in a man.
HL Mencken

*A man who doesn't trust himself can never really
trust anyone else.*
Cardinal de Retz

As contagion of sickness makes sickness,
contagion of trust makes trust.
Marianne Moore

Love all, trust a few.
Shakespeare

What loneliness is more lonely than distrust.
George Eliot

*Suspicion is a thing very few people can entertain without
letting the hypothesis turn, in their minds, into fact.*
David Cort

One never trusts anyone that one has deceived.

*Never trust a man with short legs.
Brains too near their bottoms.*
Noel Coward

Trust, but verify.

• • • • TRUTH • • • •

Baldwin occasionally stumbles over the truth, but he always hastily picks himself up and hurries on as if nothing had happened.
Winston Churchill

Truth for him was a moving target; he never aimed for the bull's eye and rarely pierced the outer ring.
Hugh Cudlipp

If you speak the truth have a foot in the stirrup.
Turkish proverb

It is always the best policy to speak the truth, unless of course, you are an exceptionally good liar.
Jerome K Jerome

What is true by lamplight is not always true by sunlight.
Joubert

Tell the truth, and so puzzle and confound your adversaries.
Sir Henry Wotton

It is the customary fate of new truths to begin as heresies and to end as superstitions.
TH Huxley

Truth needs no memory.

Platitudes are among the most useful things in the world for those who know how to use them, for truth is not the worse for being obvious, undeniable, or familiar.

It is hard to believe that a man is telling the truth when you
know that you would lie if you were in his place.
HL Mencken

*The truth would become more popular if it were not
always stating ugly facts.*

In this world, truth can wait; she's used to it.
Douglas Jerrold

If it is not true it is very well invented.

I have too much respect for the truth
to drag it out on every trifling occasion.
Mark Twain

*Something unpleasant is coming when men
are anxious to tell the truth.*
Benhamin Disraeli

Never tell a story because it is true:
tell it because it is a good story.
John Pentland Manhaffy

*Truth is a rare and precious commodity.
We must be sparing in its use.*
CP Scott

Some men love truth so much that they
seem to be in continual fear lest
she should catch a cold on over-exposure.
Samuel Butler

• • • • UNDERSTANDING • • • •

It is better to understand little than to misunderstand a lot.
Anatole France

God grant me to contend with those that understand me.
Thomas Fuller

Men are most apt to believe what they least understand.
Montaigne

He who does not understand your silence will
probably not understand your words.
Elbert Hubbard

Understanding is the beginning of approving.

Each of us really understands in others only those
feelings he is capable of producing himself.
Andre Gide

To understand everything makes one very indulgent.
Madame de Stael

Much learning does not teach understanding.
Heraclitus

• • • • UNITY • • • •

Weak things united become strong.

If a link is broken, the whole chain breaks.
Yiddish proverb

We must all hang together, or assuredly we shall all hang separately.
Benjamin Franklin

By union the smallest states thrive,
by discord the greatest are destroyed.
Sallust

All for one; one for all.
Dumas, The Three Musketeers

There are only two forces that unite men – fear and interest.
Napoleon Bonaparte

It is always possible to bind together a considerable number of people in love, so long as there are other people left over to receive the manifestations of their aggressiveness.
Sigmund Freud

• • • • UNIVERSITY • • • •

If you feel that you have both feet planted on
level ground then university has failed you.
Robert Goheen

*It (Oxford) is a sanctuary in which exploded systems and
obsolete prejudices find shelter and protection after they
have been hunted out of every corner of the world.*
Adam Smith

A professor is one who talks in someone else's sleep.
WH Auden

*What poor education I have received has been gained
in the University of Life.*
Horatio Bottomley

I was a modest, good-humoured boy.
It is Oxford that has made me insufferable.
Max Beerbohm

*A man who has never gone to school may steal from
a freight car; but if he has a university education,
he may steal the whole railroad.*
Theodore Roosevelt

I cannot see that lectures can do so much good
as reading the books from which the lectures are taken.
Samuel Johnson

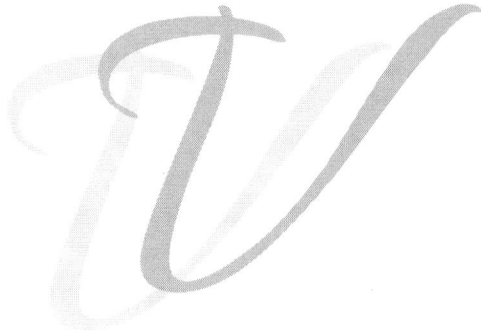

VALUE

You don't get paid for the hour.
You get paid for the value to bring to an hour.

What you really value is what you miss, not what you have.
Jorge Luis Borges

That which costs little is less valued.
Cervantes

We never know the worth of water till the well is dry.
Thomas Fuller

Everybody in the world is good for something.
At least they can be a bad example.

There is no such thing as absolute value in this world.
You can only estimate what a thing is worth to you.

What we must decide is perhaps how we are valuable
rather than how valuable we are.
Edgar Friedenberg

• • • • VISION • • • •

Vision is the art of seeing things invisible.
Jonathan Swift

*Every man takes the limits of his own field of vision
for the limits of the world.*
Schopenhauer

The vision must be followed by the venture.
It is not enough to stare up the steps.
We must step up the stairs.
Vance Hepner

*The most pathetic person in the world
is someone who has sight but no vision.*
Helen Keller

Some things have to be believed to be seen.

• • • • WEALTH • • • •

If you can actually count your money, then you're not rich.
J Paul Getty

The way to wealth is as plain as the way to market.
Benjamin Franklin

*You may try to destroy wealth and find that all you
have done is increase poverty.*
Winston Churchill

A rich man is nothing but a poor man with money.
WC Fields

Wealth can't buy health but health can buy wealth.
Thoreau

Wealth is not his that has it, but his that enjoys it.

I have been rich and I've been poor. Rich is better.
Sophie Tucker

I am opposed to millionaires but it would be
dangerous to offer me the position.
Mark Twain

He has not acquired a fortune;
the fortune has acquired him.

Prosperity is only an instrument to be used;
not a diety to be worshipped.
Calvin Coolidge

The brother had rather see the sister rich than make her so.

Heiresses are never jilted.

Poverty is an anomaly to rich people.
It is very difficult to make out why people who
want dinner do not ring the bell.
Walter Bagehot

The wretchedness of being rich is that
you live with rich people.
Logan Pearsall Smith

If Heaven had looked upon riches to be a valuable thing,
it would not have given them to such a scoundrel.
Jonathan Swift

Don't make fun of the rich.
You may be rich some day yourself.

The larger a man's roof, the more snow it collects.
Persian proverb

This is the posture of fortune's slave:
one foot in the gravy, one foot in the grave.
James Thurber

*I wish that dear Karl could have spent some time
acquiring capital instead of merely writing about it.*
Jenny Marx

No woman can be too rich or too thin.
Duchess of Windsor

*There's no reason to be the richest man in the cemetery.
You can't do business from there.*
Colonel Sanders

• • • • WINNING • • • •

Winning is a habit. Unfortunately, so is losing.

If it doesn't matter who wins, then how come they keep score?

Anyone can win – unless there happens
to be a second entry.

Winning isn't everything, but the will to win is everything.

Whoever said "It's not whether you win or lost
that counts", probably lost.

Another victory like that and we are done for.
Pyrrhus

Remember, it doesn't matter whether you win or lose;
what mattters is whether I win or lose.
Darrin Weinberg

*One should always play fairly when one
has the winning cards.*
Oscar Wilde

• • • • WISDOM • • • •

Wisdom rises upon the ruins of folly.
Thomas Fuller

He is no wise man that cannot play the fool on occasion.

How prone to doubt, how cautious are the wise!
Homer

It is very foolish to wish to be exclusively wise.

It is easier to be wise on behalf of others
then to be so for ourselves.

Nine-tenths of wisdom is to be wise in time.
Theodore Roosevelt

Youth is the time to study wisdom;
old age is the time to practise it.
Rousseau

It is characteristic of wisdom not to do desperate things.
Thoreau

It takes a wise man to recognise a wise man.

*He swallowed a lot of wisdom, but it seemed as if
all of it had gone down the wrong way.*

The farther he went west, the more convinced
he felt that the wise men came from the east.
Sydney Smith

Not by years but by disposition is wisdom acquired.
Plautus

Be wiser than other people, if you can,
but do not tell them so.
Lord Chesterfield

*Many persons might have attained the wisdom
had they not assumed that they already possessed it.*
Seneca

Knowledge comes but wisdom lingers.
Tennyson

Some are wise, some are otherwise.

● ● ● ● WIT ● ● ● ●

Wit is the power to say what everybody would like
to have said, if they had happened to think of it.
Whistler

The greatest fault of penetrating wit is to go beyond the mark.
La Rochefoucauld

Wit has truth in it; wisecracking is simply calisthenics with words.
Dorothy Parker

A man must have a good share of wit himself to endure a great share in another.
Lord Chesterfield

Even wit is a burden if it talks too long.
Latin proverb

Wit is far more often a shield than a lance.

An original wit is a guy who has heard the gag before you do.

Wit ought to be a glorious treat, like caviar: never spread it about like marmalade.
Noel Coward

An ounce of wit is worth a pound of sorrow.

Sharp wits, like sharp knives, do often cut their owners' fingers.
Arrowsmith

Wit in conversation is, in the midwives' phrase, a quick conception and an easily delivery.
Jonathan Swift

Impropriety is the soul of wit.
Somerset Maugham

Wit is the salt of conversation, not the food.
William Hazlitt

• • • • WORK • • • •

*Work is something that when we have it, we wish we didn't,
and when we don't hve it, we wish we did.*

There are many formulas for success –
but none of them work unless you do.

*He that wishes to eat the nut does not mind
cracking the shell.*
Polish proverb

When it comes to work, there are many
who will stop at nothing.

*Work is the easiest activity man has invented
to escape boredom.*

Choose a job you love, and you will never have
to work a day in your life.
Confucius

*The man who rolls up his shirt sleeves
is rarely in danger of losing his shirt.*

Work expands so as to fill the time available
for its completion.
C Northcote Parkinson

*Being busy does not always mean real work.
The object of all work is production or accomplishment
and to either of these ends there must be forethought,
system, planning, intelligence, and honest purpose
as well as perspiration. Seeming to do is not doing.*
Thomas Edison

Nobody ever drowned in his own sweat.

Work is so much more fun than fun.
Trammell Crow

The first five days of the week are when you work
to keep up with the competition. It's on Saturdays
and Sundays that you get ahead of them.
Curt Carlson

*My grandfather once told me that there were two kinds
of people: those who do the work and those who
take the credit. He told me to try to be in the first group;
there was much less competition.*
Indira Ghandi

It's always been and always will be the same in the world:
the horse does the work and the coachman is tipped.

One chops the wood, the other does the grunting.
Yiddish proverb

Work is the curse of the drinking classes.
Oscar Wilde

I like work; it fascinates me. I can sit and look at it for hours.
Jerome K Jerome

Employee: "There's no point in working late to impress
management. They all go home early".

Never itch for anything you aren't willing to scratch for.

Don't tell me how hard you work.
Tell me how much you get done.
James Ling

When your work speaks for itself, don't interrupt.
Henry Kaiser

If hard work were such a wonderful thing, surely
the rich would have kept it all to themselves.

*Hard work never killed anybody, but why take a
chance on being the first?*

Why do men delight in work? Fundamentally, I suppose,
because there is a sense of relief and pleasure in getting
something done – a kind of satisfaction not unlike
that which a hen enjoys laying an egg.
HL Mencken

Work is the refuge of people who have nothing better to do.
Oscar Wilde

Robinson Crusoe started the forty-hour week.
He had all his work done by Friday.

*Nothing is really work unless you would rather
be doing something else.*
Sir James Barrie

The difference between a job and a career is the
difference between forty and sixty hours a week.
Robert Frost

I am a friend of the working man, and I would rather be a friend than be one.
Clarence Darrow

• • • • WORRY • • • •

Worry is the interest paid on trouble before it falls due.

An activity as useless as whispering in a boiler factory.

If you want to test your memory, try to remember what you were worrying about one year ago today.

Wear your worries like a loose garment.

If you must worry, don't worry out loud. It wastes the time of others as well as your own.

Keep cool: it will be all one a hundred years hence.
Ralph Waldo Emerson

The longer we dwell on our misfortunes the greater is their power to harm us.
Voltaire

It is not work that kills men; it is worry. Worry is rust upon the blade.
Henry Ward Beecher

Z

• • • • ZEAL • • • •

What wins out when ability falters.

Zeal without knowledge is fire without light.
Thomas Fuller

Let a man in a garret but burn with intensity
and he will set fire to the world.

935-). American film actor, writer and director.

s (1894-1984). American drama critic and essayist.

1860-1937). Scottish dramatist and novelist.

n, Bernard (1870-1965). American businessman and statesman.

Beecham, Sir Thomas (1879 -1961). English conductor.

Beerbohm, Sir Max (1872-1956). English essayist and caricaturist.

Bierce, Ambrose (1842-1914). American journalist, short-story writer, poet.

Billings, Josh (1818-1885). American humorist.

Byron, Lord (1788-1824). English poet.

Carnegie, Dale (1888-1955). American author and lecturer.

Carroll, Lewis. *Pen name of Charles Lutwidge Dodson* (1832-1898). English writer and mathematician.

Cervantes, Miguel de (1547-1616). Spanish novelist, dramatist, poet.

Chesterfield, Lord (1694-1773). English statesman and man of letters.

Chesterton, GK (1874-1936). English journalist, essayist, novelist, poet.

Colton, Charles Caleb (1780-1832). English writer and clergyman.

Coward, Noel (1899-1973). English playwright, actor, composer.

Disraeli, Benjamin (1804-1881). English statesman and novelist.

Dostoevsky, Fyodor (1821-1881). Russian writer.

Edison, Thomas Alva (1847-1931). American inventor.

Einstein, Albert (1879-1955). German-Swiss-American physicist.

Emerson, Ralph Waldo (1803-1882). American poet, essayist, philosopher.

Fields, WC (1880-1946). American humorist.

Franklin, Benjamin (1706-1790). American statesman, writer, inventor, printer, scientist.

Gide, Andre (1869-1951). French novelist, essayist, critic, editor, translator.

Goethe, Johann Wolfgang von (1749-1832). German poet, playwright, novelist.

Goldwyn, Sam (1882-1974). Polish-born American film producer.

Hammarskjold, Dag (1905-1961). Swedish statesman, secretary-general of the United Nations.

Hazlitt, William (1778-1830). English essayist and critic.

Heine, Heinrich (1797-1856). German poet, satirist, journalist.

Heraclitus (c 500BC). Greek philosopher.

Hoffer, Eric (1902-1983). American philosopher and author.

Howe, Edgar Watson (1853-1937). American editor, author, essayist.

Hubbard, Elbert (1856-1915). American businessman, writer, printer.

Huxley, Thomas Henry (1825-1895). English biologist, teacher, writer.

Jefferson, Thomas (1743-1826). American statesman, third president of the United States.

Jerome, Jerome K (1859-1927). English novelist and playwright.

Jerrold, Douglas (1803-1857). English playwright and humorist.

Johnson, Samuel (1709-1784). English lexicographer, essayist, poet, wit.

Kant, Immanuel (1724-1804). German philosopher.

Krutch, Joseph Wood (1893-1970). American essayist, critic, teacher.

La Rochefoucauld, Francois, Duc de (1613-1680). French writer.

Lippmann, Walter (1889-1974). American newspaper columnist and author.

Macaulay, Thomas Babington, 1st Baron Macaulay (1800-1859). English statesman, poet, historian, biographer.

Marquis, Donald (1878-1937). American newspaperman and humorist.

Martial *(full name Marcus Valerius Martialis)* (AD 42-102). Latin poet born in Spain.

Maugham, Somerset (1874-1965). English novelist and playwright.

Mencken, HL (1880-1956). American newspaperman, editor, writer.

Montaigne, Michel (1533-1592). French moralist and essayist.

Nietzsche, Friedrich (1844-1900). German philosopher.

Parker, Dorothy (1893-1967). American writer of short stories, verse, criticism.

Parkinson, C Northcote (1909-1993). American historian and writer.

Perelman, SJ (1904-1979). American humorist.

Plautus *(full name Titus Maccius Plautus)* (254-184 BC). Roman comic playwright.

Rogers, Will (1879-1935). American actor and humorist.

Russell, Bertrand, 3rd Earl Russell (1872-1970). English philosopher, mathematician, social reformer.

Santayana, George (1863-1952). Spanish-born American philosopher, poet, novelist, critic.

Schopenhauer, Arthur (1788-1860). German philosopher.

Seneca *(full name Lucius Annaeus Seneca)* (55 BC - AD 39). Roman rhetorician.

Shaw, George Bernard (1856-1950). Irish playwright, critic, social reformer.

Swift, Jonathan (1667-1745). English satirist.

Tennyson, Alfred, 1st Baron Tennyson (1809-1892). English poet.

Thoreau, Henry David (1817-1862). American essayist, naturalist, poet.

Tocqueville, Count Alexis de (1805-1859). French political leader, historian, writer.

Twain, Mark. *Pen name of Samuel Langhorne Clemens* (1835-1910). American writer and humorist.

Voltaire. *Pen name of Francois Marie Arouet* (1694-1778). French satirist, essayist, dramatist, philosopher, historian.

Whitehead, Alfred North (1861-1947). British philospher, mathematician.

Wilde, Oscar (1854-1900). Irish-born English poet, playwright, novelist, wit.

Wotton, Sir Henry (1568-1639). English diplomat and poet.

• • • • YOUR OWN QUOTES • • • •

You may like to use this page to jot down some quotes of your own – bon mots which you don't want to lose!

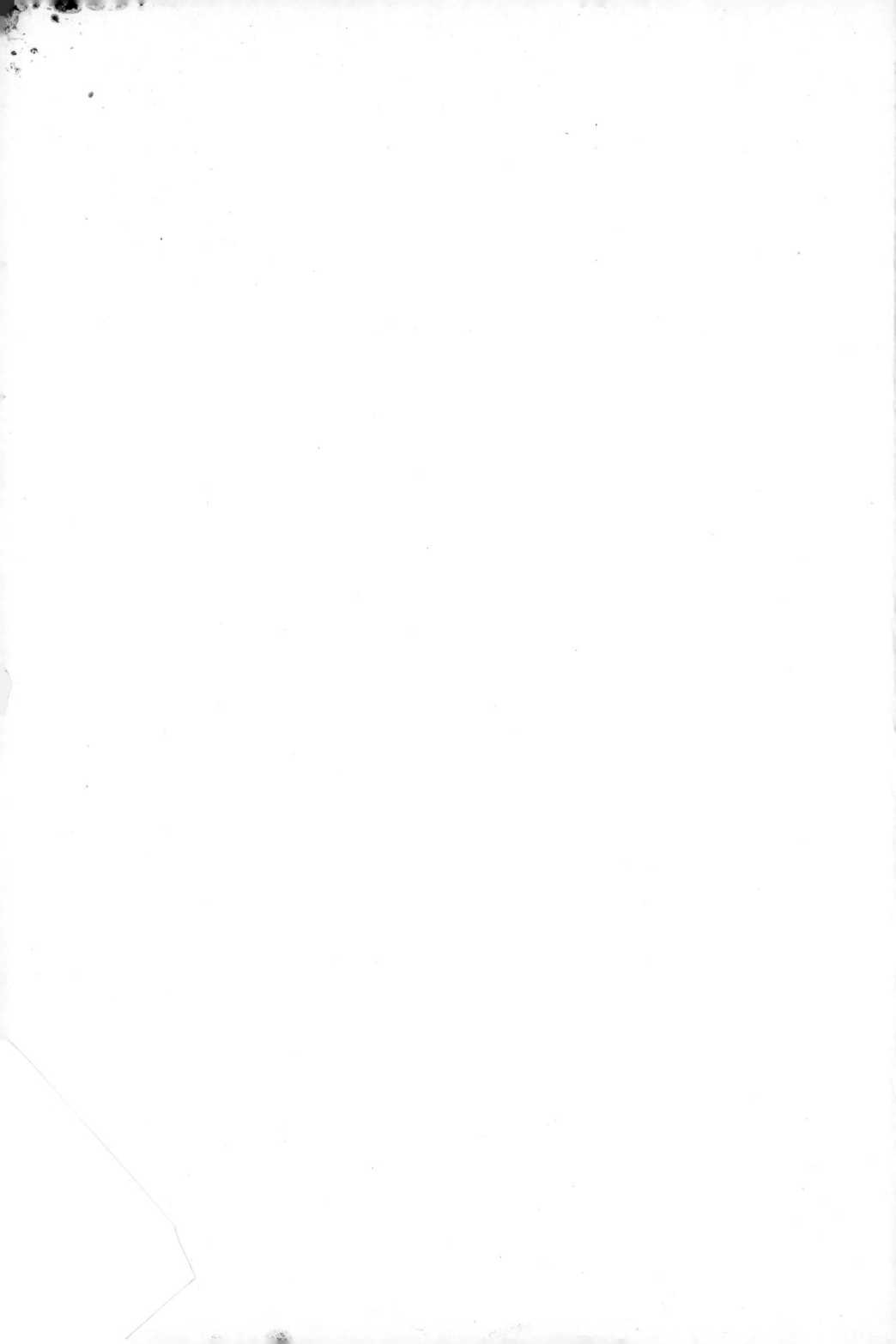